ALONE *in the* APPALACHIANS

D1605166

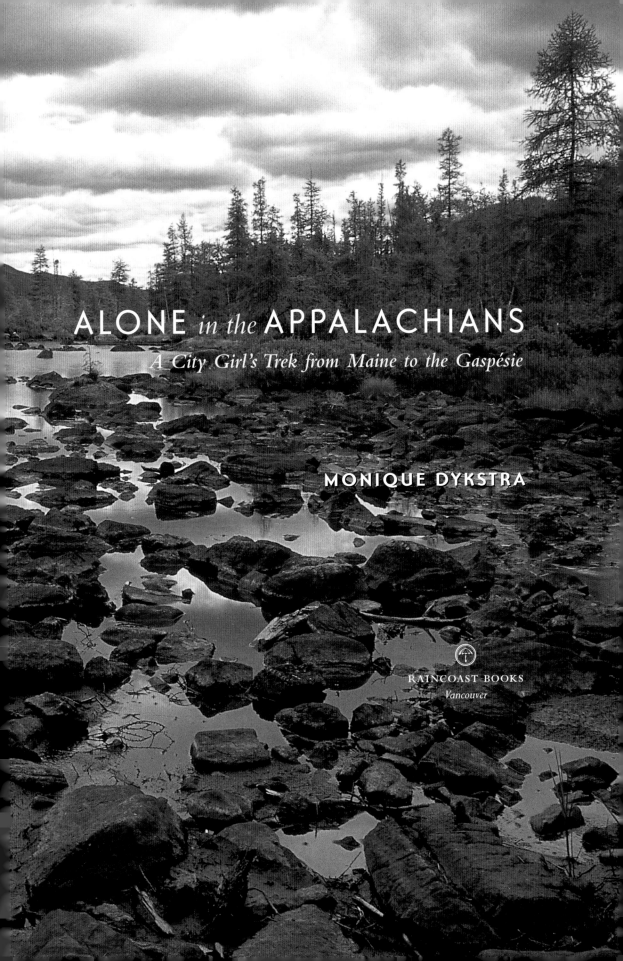

ALONE *in the* APPALACHIANS

A City Girl's Trek from Maine to the Gaspésie

MONIQUE DYKSTRA

RAINCOAST BOOKS

Vancouver

THIS IS A RAINCOAST JOURNEYS BOOK

Text copyright © 2001 by Monique Dykstra
All photographs copyright © 2001 by Monique Dykstra, except for the following:
SEPAQ-Parc de la Gaspésie pages 6, 11, 22, 31, 58, 102, 110-11, 119 bottom, 127; Portland
Press Herald/Maine Sunday Telegram, staff photo by Gregory Rec, pages 23, 86, 90; Parc
National Forillon, pages 106 (Jean-Guy Beliveau), 134 (Jean Audet), 135 (Suzie Roy), 138-39
(Pierre St-Jacques); Claude Bouchard pages 98-99.
Maps © Jim Miller/fennana design

All rights reserved. No part of this publication may be reproduced or transmitted in any
form or by any means, electronic or mechanical, including photocopying, recording or
by any information storage and retrieval system now known or to be invented, without
permission in writing from the publisher.

Raincoast Books gratefully acknowledges the ongoing support of the Canada Council for
the Arts; the British Columbia Arts Council; and the Government of Canada through the
Department of Canadian Heritage Book Publishing Industry Development Program
(BPIDP).

Edited by Scott Steedman

National Library of Canada Cataloguing in Publication Data

Dykstra, Monique, 1964-
   Alone in the Appalachians

   Includes bibliographical references and index.
   ISBN 1-55192-477-3

   1. Dykstra, Monique, 1964- —Journeys—Appalachian Trail. 2. Appalachian Trail—
Description and travel. 3. Hiking—Appalachian Trail. I. Title.
F106.D99 2002   917.404'44   C2001-911686-1

Raincoast Books
9050 Shaughnessy Street
Vancouver, British Columbia
Canada, V6P 6E5
www.raincoast.com

Printed and bound in Hong Kong.

1 2 3 4 5 6 7 8 9 10

Cover photo: *The distinctive Pic du Brûlé, seen from Pic du l'Aube, in Quebec's
   Parc de la Gaspésie*
Pages 2–3: *Brooding clouds over Lac du Diable (Devil Lake) in Quebec's Parc de la Gaspésie*
Back cover: *Stealth camping in a Maine farmer's field*

For Saeb, because you never did get to see the trail for yourself

▲ *Moose tracks beside Lac Cascapédia in Quebec's Parc de la Gaspésie*

CONTENTS

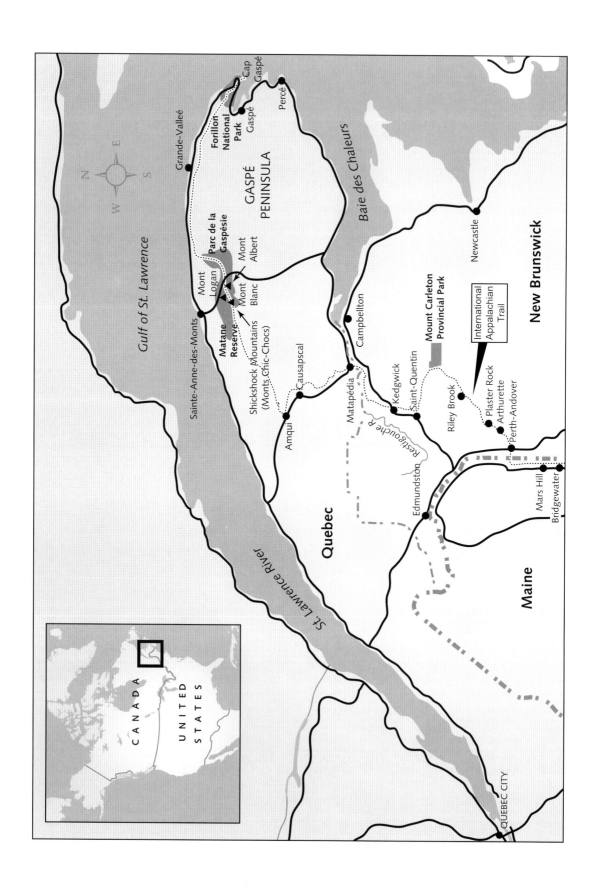

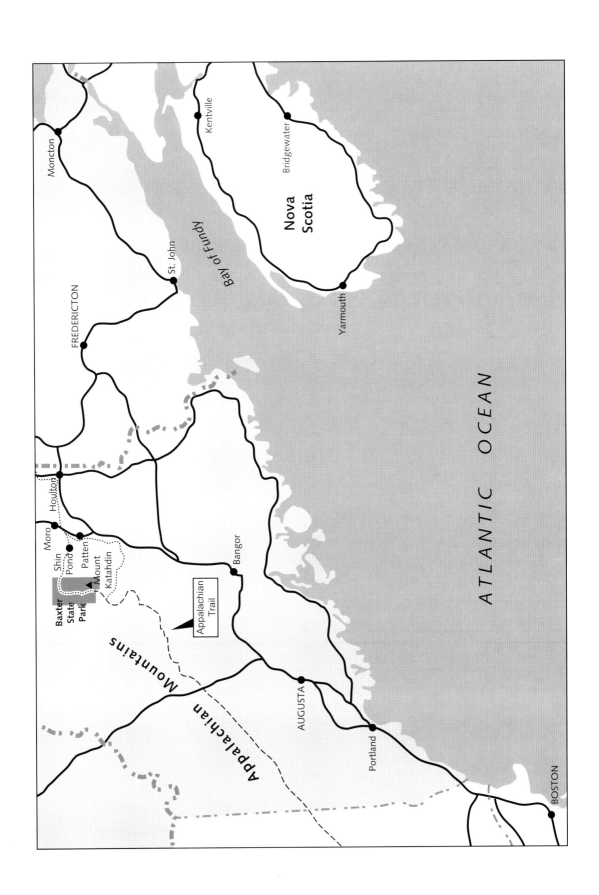

▲ *Glistening rocks and falling water in Quebec's Matane Reserve*

Foreword

The International Appalachian Trail (*Sentier International des Appalaches*) connects countries, states and provinces, mountains and parks — and it connects people. Monique Dykstra's journey along the IAT truly represents the spirit and philosophy of such a long-distance hiking trail.

Hikers give life and vitality to a trail. They provide the spiritual connections between people and places and turn a path in the woods into a living entity. In her journey, Monique has fulfilled the purpose of the IAT — giving people an opportunity to celebrate the grandeur of the Northern Appalachian landscape that is shared by Canada and the United States.

Monique's trek from Maine's Katahdin through New Brunswick's northern forest, then east through Quebec's Gaspé Peninsula to spectacular Cap Gaspé, is her very own epic. Her trials and tribulations, joys and rewards are woven into a wonderful story for all to enjoy. Her telling of the story at once rewards the builders of the trail, provides a small measure of immortality to the trail, and is a tribute to her perseverance and determination.

Dick Anderson
President and founder of the International Appalachian Trail

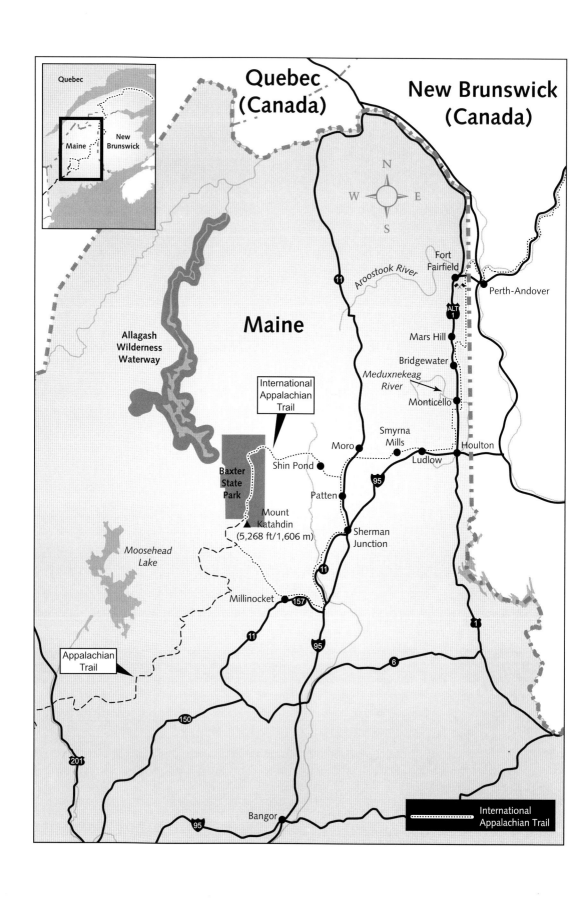

Quebec
(Canada)

New Brunswick
(Canada)

Maine

Allagash
Wilderness
Waterway

Aroostook River

Fort
Fairfield

Perth-Andover

ALT
1

Mars Hill

Bridgewater

Meduxnekeag
River

Monticello

International
Appalachian
Trail

Smyrna
Mills

Moro

Houlton

Shin Pond

Ludlow

Baxter
State
Park

95

Patten

Mount
Katahdin
(5,268 ft/1,606 m)

Sherman
Junction

Moosehead
Lake

11

Millinocket

157

Appalachian
Trail

11

95

6

1

150

201

Bangor

95

International
Appalachian Trail

Prologue

High-rises. Traffic jams. Neighbours who crank up the dance tunes at 3:00 a.m., forcing you to get up, shuffle outside, ring the bell and scream at the top of your lungs when they open the door. This was the life that I knew.

Taking a solitary 1,000-kilometre stroll through the woods, this I knew little about.

I'd always wanted to do a long-distance hike. I didn't know much about hiking, but I didn't tell Raincoast Books that. At the time, I was too busy trying to sell them the idea of doing a book on the International Appalachian Trail, or IAT. I mean, how difficult could it be? Wasn't hiking simply a matter of throwing some clothes and a few granola bars into a backpack and heading for the hills?

Ha!

▲ *Roadside artwork spotted near Baxter State Park*

MAINE
The Adventure Begins

I left for my IAT hike on July 27, 2000. Picking up my backpack, I took a final look around the apartment: last night's dishes neatly stacked in the dish tray, the humming fridge, the warm glow of the lamp on the kitchen table.

Terror was lodged in my throat like a burr. Why was I doing this? Why leave everything behind to fall headlong into fear? I couldn't think of a single reason, but I closed the door, took a taxi downtown and boarded the bus for Woodstock, New Brunswick.

On the bus, I ignored the highway, the sunny fields, the cloud-dotted sky. I ignored the waving purple wildflowers, my fellow passengers and every passing hour. I figured if I ignored everything, then I wasn't really there, so I couldn't worry about hiking the IAT.

Then, all too soon, I arrived in Woodstock, where I was to meet Mel Fitton, a member of the local IAT chapter. There's no bus service to Baxter Park in nearby Maine where the IAT begins, so Mel had generously offered to drive me there.

Within four minutes of shaking my hand, Mel cleared his throat, looked me straight in the eye and said: "Did you know that two women were murdered on the Appalachian Trail a few years back?"

Mel Fitton was the first of about 10,000 people to imply that I was crazy to hike the IAT alone as a woman.

The Appalachian Trail

The IAT is the Canadian extension of North America's most popular hiking trail, the Appalachian Trail. Almost 3,500 kilometres long, the Appalachian Trail meanders along the backbone of the Appalachian Mountain chain from Springer Mountain, Georgia, to Mount Katahdin, Maine.

The Appalachian Trail was the vision of E. Benton MacKaye, a mild-mannered civil servant with the U.S. government in the 1920s. Hidden behind stacks of papers in his dusty cubicle, MacKaye dreamt of a long-distance hike that would run along the tips of the Appalachian Mountains.

But MacKaye didn't just dream about hikers. His trail would link a series of farms, work camps and study centres, where urban workers could escape the tensions of industrialisation in the crisp mountain air. Eventually, these camps would become co-operative mountaintop communities where the citizens would support themselves with "non-industrial activity."

The mountaintop communities never got past MacKaye's cubicle, but the trail certainly did: it's estimated that three to four million people use the Appalachian Trail each year. Most only hike for a day or two, but over six thousand people have hiked the trail from start to finish since its inception.

The International Appalachian Trail

"Yup, it's a great trail," thought retired Maine Commissioner of Conservation Dick Anderson while stuck in a traffic jam in 1994. "But it could be better."

Why did the Appalachian Trail stop in northern Maine when the Appalachian Mountains kept on going? Why not continue the trail from Mount Katahdin through northern Maine, across New Brunswick, then finish where the Appalachian Mountains plunge into the sea at the tip of the Gaspé Peninsula in Quebec?

Anderson envisioned a new hiking trail that would "connect mountains, cross rivers, thread through spruce and fir forests, and connect people and cultures." The IAT would be a model of international co-operation, with the goal of protecting a common environment. And like its big brother, the Appalachian Trail, the IAT would be built and maintained by volunteers.

It took six years to build the IAT. While there's still much work to be done, IAT president and founder Dick Anderson declared the 1,000-kilometre trail complete on Earth Day, 2000.

While "complete" means finished, it doesn't mean a complete wilderness experience. Much of the IAT is still along public roadways. That's because it takes vast amounts of time and money to persuade landowners that turning over large tracts of their land to a band of grimy hikers is a great — even admirable — idea. Also, hikers usually want the land cheap, preferably free. This generally produces big belly laughs around boardroom tables and little else — which is why it took seventy-five years to build the original Appalachian Trail.

Baxter Park

The IAT starts where the Appalachian Trail finishes — one vertical mile straight up, on Mount Katahdin's windy summit in Baxter Park.

I was crying after hiking to the top of Katahdin. It was beautiful: mountains, deserted valleys and unbroken forest as far as the eye could see, streaks of pink and yellow criss-crossing the sky, and far, far below, the silver threads of rivers glinting in the sun.

But it wasn't the beauty that moved me to tears — it was my feet. My new hiking boots had chewed them to bits. Plus the sun was going down, which meant I had to hobble back down the mountain in order to reach bottom by dark.

I'd originally planned to climb Mount Katahdin, camp for the night, then spend three days hiking north through Baxter Park. This was one of the two routes suggested by the IAT through this section of Maine. The other route involved climbing Katahdin, walking back down and then trudging along the road.

I wasn't interested in road walking, so I had called the park six weeks in advance for camping reservations. The woman on the phone just laughed. "We were sold out by March," she said. "Try again next year." That wasn't an option, so my plan was to climb Katahdin, sneak through the park and camp wherever I could. My plan had collapsed thirty steps down the trail.

"That's a pretty big backpack you got there. Camping in the park?" inquired the soft-spoken ranger, who seemed to appear out of nowhere.

"Who me?" I answered.

"Can I see your permit?" he asked.

When he found out I didn't have one, rather than getting angry, he offered to radio headquarters to ask if there were any campsite vacancies in the park.

I wandered around the ranger's hut while he fiddled with the radio. No answer. He tried again. No answer. He leaned back in his chair, tipped his cap back and looked out the window. Without looking at me, the ranger gently explained that unauthorised camping is prohibited in Baxter Park to protect its pristine wilderness.

"If you sneak through," he said, "then everyone else would do it, and eventually the park would be ruined for everyone."

The ranger suggested that I leave my pack at the ranger station, hike to the top of Katahdin that day, then follow the alternate IAT route along the road.

Mount Katahdin

At first I was disappointed, but I soon realized that getting nabbed by the ranger was

a stroke of luck. Climbing Katahdin involves hauling yourself over car-sized boulders, squeezing through rocky crevices and tip-toeing across knife-edged peaks. It was hard enough hauling my lunch to the summit, let alone an enormous backpack.

The highest point in Maine, Katahdin towers above surrounding peaks like a giant among dwarves. It's also remote — so remote that for several hundred years, few non-natives could even find it. Among those who tried and failed was Henry David Thoreau.

▲ *The IAT begins one vertical mile straight up, on Mount Katahdin's windy summit.*

Descending Mount Katahdin, the first few steps of the IAT are treacherous but exhilarating. ▶

In Thoreau's day, there were no trails through the dense woods surrounding the mountain. Fighting through the bush was too difficult, so Thoreau took a boat up the Penobscot River, then followed a stream uphill until it petered out. From there, he took a compass bearing, crashed around in the woods for a while, then gave up in disgust. He had no idea where he was, and swirling clouds had reduced his visibility to nil. In fact, Thoreau was just 400 metres below the summit when he turned back.

Officially, the summit remained unclimbed until 1804, when a man named Charles Turner, Jr. finally reached the top.

The local Penobscot Indians probably reached the summit long before Turner, but as a general rule, they avoided the mountain like the plague. The Penobscots believed that Katahdin was home to the evil god Pamola. Pamola was believed to kidnap hunters and warriors who strayed too close to the summit. Held hostage beneath the mountain, the men were forced to wed the god's unmarried sisters and daughters. When finally allowed to go home, the warriors left Katahdin with Pamola's warning ringing in their ears: stay away from all women, or risk vanishing beneath the mountain forever.

Pamola was nowhere to be seen the day I climbed Katahdin. Instead, I was plagued by an evil spirit of a different sort: self-doubt.

For this book, I had proposed a personal account of hiking the IAT. But self-reflection is much like belly laughter — hollow if forced and hard to do on demand. What if I didn't have a single profound thought for two months? Because really, how much could a person write about walking down a trail?

Worrying about thinking proved to be more tiring than walking. Soon, I was lying on my back in the middle of the path. Over my laboured breathing, I heard a waterfall tumbling over boulders in the distance. The sun through the leaves cast lacy shadows on the path. I moved my head into a patch of sunshine and closed my eyes. The wind was a soft whisper through the trees. Nothing profound here — nothing but wind, sun and dappled forest. Nothing. And that's exactly what Percival Baxter had in mind when he created this park.

Percival Baxter

As governor of Maine in the 1920s, Baxter had tried persuading the legislature to set aside Mount Katahdin and surrounding lands for public use. When the legislature refused, Baxter pulled out his wallet and bought the mountain, along with 2,500 hectares of wilderness. He donated the land to the state of Maine and was attacked as a dreamer and branded a socialist for his efforts.

Upon bestowing his gift, Baxter's only conditions were that the land be turned into a park, and that it be left "forever wild." He believed that "… as modern civilization with its trailers, its hot dog stands, its radio and its jazz, encroaches on the Maine wilderness, the time may yet come when only the Katahdin region remains undefiled by man."

Not content with buying the tallest mountain in Maine and a great swath of wilderness, Baxter bought an additional 80,000 hectares of land over the next few decades. All of this, as well as operating funds, was donated to the state of Maine.

Today, the operating staff of Baxter Park remains faithful to Baxter's vision. There are no phones, no showers, no water fountains, no electricity, no hamburger stands and no hotels in the park. Also prohibited are motor homes, trailers, motorcycles, motorboats, trail bikes, pets, radios and televisions.

Take a walk in the woods — that's all there is to do in Baxter Park. For company, you'll have bear, moose, deer and even the occasional bobcat. There are spectacular vistas, cascading waterfalls, steep gorges and, best of all, a sense of infinite wilderness.

What a park. What a man. And surprisingly, what a poet:

Man is born to die. His works are short-lived.
Buildings crumble, monuments decay, wealth vanishes.
But Katahdin, in all its glory, forever shall remain
The mountain of the people of Maine.

Percival Baxter

Today, that sense of wilderness survives only within the confines of Baxter Park. Strip malls and satellite dishes loom just beyond the park gates.

Millinocket

After climbing Katahdin, I left the park and headed for Millinocket. As I marched along the winding country road, my thoughts ranged from "Why am I doing this?" to "My feet are sore" to "Wow, my pack is heavy." This whirl of nonsense was occasionally interrupted by passing motorists, who would screech to a stop, stick their heads out the window and ask if I wanted a ride.

"Thanks a lot, just out walking for the pleasure of it," I'd reply. The moment they pulled away, the wild horses returned.

In normal life, our minds are fed by an uninterrupted stream of information. Newspapers, magazines, TV, the internet — we leap from one stimulus to the next, ever in search of New! Interesting! Exciting! Now imagine taking all that great stuff away and replacing it with a murderously heavy backpack, a pair of stiff new hiking boots and over a thousand kilometres of trail stretching out in front of you.

▲ *Squaring a beam on one of the IAT's many new overnight shelters*

In total, seven vehicles stopped to offer me a ride into Millinocket. The last one was the hardest to resist. Moments before he stopped, I'd just crawled out of the ditch where I'd been examining my bleeding feet.

Hiking books always tell you to break in your boots before leaving for a trip. If you don't have time, these books cheerily instruct you to submerge your new boots in the bathtub, then clomp around in them until they're dry.

I'd tried. I'd run the bath, taken my gorgeous new boots out of the box, and held them above the steaming water. I'd tried lowering them in, but my arm wouldn't budge. These were my dream hiking boots. Italian leather. Hand-stitched by some wizened cobbler in a Sicilian village, no doubt. Thick-soled and heavy, the boots looked strong enough to handle anything from the Everglades to Everest.

◀ *Close encounter with a white-tailed deer*

Rather than soaking my boots in the bathtub, I'd carefully wrapped them in tissue, stowed them in the box and forgotten about them until the day I started my IAT hike.

Big mistake.

All the way to Millinocket, it felt like I was walking on broken glass. As for my skin, it felt like that wizened cobbler had lined my boots with eighty-grit sandpaper rather than leather.

"Thanks, but I'm just out walking for fun," I answered when the last vehicle stopped. I waved until they disappeared around a bend. Then, very slowly, I started walking again. For fun.

I camped at the Big Moose Campground that night, a few kilometres outside Millinocket. When I woke up the next morning, it felt like someone had bashed my head with a brick, jumped all over my body in a pair of army boots, and then cut my tendons with a rusty razor blade. I nearly fell over when I got out of the tent — my legs simply refused to bend. Staggering around the campsite, it occurred to me that I'd never felt worse in my life.

Coffee. That was what I needed. I pulled the stove out of my pack, pumped it up and held a match to the jet. Nothing. I pumped some more, lit another match and tried again. Nothing. I shook the fuel bottle, pumped some more and tried again.

In addition to advising you to baptize your new boots in the bathtub, hiking books also suggest that you test your gear before you go. The stove had worked like a charm on my balcony. Out here in hiker hell, though, it simply wasn't co-operating. I abandoned it, swallowed four aspirins and staggered off to the shower.

The shower was a good idea — it cleared my head and lifted the blanket of pain. I got a take-out coffee from the campground store, ate a bowl of cold oatmeal, packed up my gear and left.

I arrived in Millinocket in late afternoon. As a reward for surviving the first portion of my journey, I decided to treat myself to a hotel that night.

The AT Lodge is at the end of Millinocket's main street. It was once a boarding house for local mill workers, but current owners Don and Joan Cogswell started opening their doors to backpackers when layoffs at the mill resulted in empty beds.

A rambling red house with lace curtains at the windows, the AT Lodge is a backpacker's shrine. Upstairs, where the hikers stay, the halls are crowded with ghosts of hikers past. The walls are lined with backpacking paraphernalia, including maps, letters, photographs and newspaper clippings. There's even an Earl Shaeffer room, in honour of the first person to hike the Appalachian Trail in one uninterrupted trek, in 1948. Shaeffer hiked the trail again in 1965, then again in 1998, commenting that he was "mighty, mighty, mighty glad" to be finished his third and final hike. He was a month shy of his eightieth birthday at the time.

The Cogswells live downstairs at the AT Lodge. Don Cogswell, a lanky man in his early seventies, insisted on feeding me cough syrup as I paid him for the room. I'd been coughing all day. Pocketing the money, Cogswell crossed the living room into the kitchen, leaving me to admire a pair of snowshoes decorated with moose scenes and a paint-by-numbers scene of Katahdin.

"I'm a psychiatrist, I'm a doctor, I'm a dad to these hikers," said Cogswell, handing me the medicine bottle. Easing himself into a nearby recliner, he started talking about some of the backpackers he'd met over the years.

In addition to Shaeffer, Cogswell had great respect for Eb "Nimblewill Nomad" Eberhart, a retired optometrist from Georgia. Nimblewill walked from Key West, Florida, to Cap Gaspé, Quebec, in 1998. That trail, unofficially dubbed the Eastern Continental Trail (ECT), is over 7,000 kilometres long. Walking ten million steps is an accomplishment in itself, but that trip also gave Nimblewill the distinction of being one of the first people to hike the IAT.

Nimblewill enjoyed long-distance hiking so much that he walked the entire ECT again in 2000, this time in reverse. In fact, I had just missed meeting him. Nimblewill had stayed at the AT Lodge after finishing the IAT a few weeks earlier. After a short rest, he'd headed south on the Appalachian Trail (I later learned that Nimblewill reached Key West in April 2001).

"I admire these people, I really do," Cogswell said. "Long-distance hiking takes a special kind of person. No way I could do it."

I wasn't sure I could do it either. I'd only walked fifty kilometres so far, and it had nearly killed me.

In *The Advanced Backpacker*, veteran hiker Chris Townsend writes that "Carrying a [heavy] load is one of the biggest causes of misery for many long-distance hikers." The rule of thumb is that one's backpack should weigh about one-quarter of one's body weight.

When I weighed my pack at the AT Lodge, I was horrified to discover that it weighed thirty kilos (that's 66 pounds for the metric-impaired, and just for the record, I don't weigh 264 pounds). Photography gear, all of which I needed, accounted for five kilos. But I could live without my cell phone, a plate, an extra fuel bottle, a spare T-shirt and a few pairs of socks.

The pack was still too heavy, so out came the wool toque, a heavy pocket knife and a bag of parsley flakes. The parsley didn't weigh much, but getting rid of it made me feel like a hardened long-distance hiker.

I packed the spare gear into a box, then headed downtown to mail everything home.

Timber Fever

There was a painting of an old-time log drive on the wall in the Millinocket post office. The picture was of a rushing river, jammed with logs from side to side. Burly lumberjacks lined the riverbanks, watching the sea of wood careen down the river.

The scene had a mythical quality to it, and spoke of a long-ago era when brashness, vitality and adventure pumped through the veins of men. But what the painting failed to show was how tough the life really was.

In the 1800s, logging took place in the winter months, deep in the frigid woods. Home was a crude log building with a dirt floor and gaping hole in the roof for ventilation. The men slept on rough pallets, directly on the ground. The greatest challenge was in keeping clothes dry during the damp days and icy nights.

Waking at dawn, the loggers forced their feet into frozen boots, washed down bowls of beans with mugs of molasses tea, then headed off to work. Each man had a different task. The "choppers" felled the trees, the "teamsters" hauled the logs with teams of draft animals, and the "yard men" unloaded the logs and stacked them in piles on the riverbank. When the spring thaw came, the logs were rolled in the river, and the "log drivers" took over.

The log drivers were the cowboys of the lumber trade, the ones who oversaw the drives. Their job was to leap from tree to tree as the slippery logs shot down the river through a series of floating dams. When the logs reached a dam, the doors were opened, and the wood — topped by dripping wet loggers wearing

The Appalachian Trail Café, the preferred hangout for many long-distance hikers in Millinocket, Maine ▲

red-checked shirts — shot through the sluice and floated down to the next reservoir.

A clean drive meant getting all the logs to the sawmill, something that rarely happened. Low water made it difficult to move the logs, while high water flung the wood high and dry. Injury and death were regular occurrences. Hopping around on the logs, men inevitably broke their legs, banged their heads, even fell in the river and drowned.

The men harvested many different kinds of trees, but white pine was most common. The tallest, straightest pine logs went to England for the ever-expanding Royal Navy.

In the 1600s, England was desperate for lumber for shipbuilding. Europe's forests had long since been depleted, so when vast stands of "mast trees" were discovered in the New World, England promptly established the "Broad Arrow Policy" of 1691. This (rather presumptuous) law decreed that trees measuring over sixty centimetres in diameter and growing within five kilometres of water belonged to the Royal Navy. Such trees were blazed with the "broad arrow," which was how the term "King's Pine" was coined.

As the lumber trade grew, so did land speculation. With land selling at ridiculous prices in the early 1800s, so many people rushed to the nearby town of Bangor that hotel rooms were often unavailable. In 1835, the *Eastern Argus* carried a story about a young traveller so desperate for a place to stay that he paid seventy-five cents just to lean against a signpost.

The land boom ended in Maine as abruptly as it began, but the lumber trade continued to flourish. In 1899, the Great Northern Paper Company opened a large mill in Millinocket. Within a year, over 2,000 people had moved to the area, including an eclectic mix of French-Canadians, Lithuanians, Poles, Estonians, Russians and Germans.

A century later, the Great Northern Paper Company is still an important employer in Millinocket, though uncertainties in the paper industry have caused layoffs in recent years.

"Millinocket's a ghost town now," a woman in line at the post office confided. "I got laid off last year. I'll be leavin' town soon."

I too had to be leaving town, so I mailed the box and left the post office. But before leaving, I had to get something to eat.

Bear from Atlanta

The Appalachian Trail Café was at the end of the downtown strip. I was just finishing my meal when Bear from Atlanta walked in, approached my table, and asked if he could sit down.

As a nickname, "Bear" seemed a bit of a misnomer. This hiker was a slight man with smooth skin, manicured nails and hiking pants with sharp creases down the legs.

Prior to tackling the Appalachian Trail, Bear had never been hiking before. Everything he knew, he had learned on the internet. After three years of research, Bear ordered all the best gear that money could buy: a down sleeping bag, an ultralight stove, a set of titanium cooking pots. He even bought his backpack over the phone — some exotic custom-made affair. The clerk was reluctant to sell it to him. "You really should try it on before spending all that money," he pleaded. But Bear was not to be dissuaded. Nothing but the best would do.

In addition to his essential gear, Bear loaded up with dozens of sundry items such as a backpacker's oven, a deluxe candle lantern and a global positioning system. His final purchase was fourteen bottles of vitamins.

Once everything was assembled, Bear quit his job and bought a one-way ticket from Atlanta to Boston, the closest major city to the trailhead. But somehow he missed his plane, and the ticket wasn't refundable. It would have cost too much to buy another plane ticket, so he hopped on a bus. Two days into the trip, he was loitering in the toilet during a pit stop when the bus roared away without him.

When he finally caught up with his pack, most of his gear had been stolen. Bear re-ordered everything, got back on the bus, and finally arrived in Millinocket two weeks later.

After a few days' rest, he loaded up his pack and caught a ride to Baxter Park and the start of the Appalachian Trail. Ten steps down the path, Bear realized that the enormous backpack he'd bought wouldn't stay on his narrow shoulders, despite his desperate (and completely random) tugging at the multitude of straps. Plus, his legs seemed to have a mind of their own. Rather than proceeding forward, they remained firmly planted on the path, while his knees bucked uncontrollably under the horrendous weight of his pack.

Bear retraced his steps, hitchhiked back into Millinocket, entered the Appalachian

Café, headed for my table, asked if he could sit down, and out tumbled the whole miserable story.

After much sympathetic clucking on my part, I paid for my meal and returned to the AT Lodge to pack my gear. An hour later, I peered through the restaurant window as I was leaving town. Bear was still sitting there, one leg jitterbugging under the table, fingers drumming on the tabletop and eyes zigzagging from side to side.

I never saw Bear again, though I thought about him obsessively for the rest of the day. Unable to hike the Appalachian Trail, and probably unwilling to slink home, Bear was stranded in a café in northern Maine with only his crushed dreams for company. I couldn't imagine a worse fate.

Romance Novels

After Baxter Park, most of the IAT follows public roadways in Maine. Even though I knew this, I didn't fully understand what this meant until leaving Millinocket.

I passed a string of shopping malls. Tractor-trailers thundered past, spewing dust and grinding gears. Heat flickered in waves off the pavement. Carloads of people flashed by, their faces pressed against the air-conditioned windows, staring out at me. After twenty minutes, I'd had enough. I threw the pack down, zipped open the top pocket, and pulled out a book.

Novel in hand, I shouldered the pack again and resumed walking. Suddenly the trucks, the big-box stores, the staring faces vanished as I tumbled into a world of steaming kisses, heaving bodices and rich, mysterious men.

Romance novels. That's how I got through the state of Maine.

With my nose pressed into the book, the kilometres flew beneath my feet. Soon I was crossing a bridge over the Penobscot River. The turnoff for Route 11 North was just past the bridge. I left the highway and headed down the winding country road. Houses were scarce along here, and cars even scarcer. Except for the squeak of my new boots and the throaty cries of crickets, it was blissfully quiet for over an hour.

Then a car roared past. Loud music spewed out the open window. I caught a glimpse of a tattooed forearm before the car disappeared around a bend.

That's when I panicked.

What if that car had screeched to a stop? What if a mad rapist had leapt out and attacked me? What if — what if —

I left the road and ran through the woods. A few seconds later, I stumbled upon the Penobscot River. I threw my pack down, tore off my boots and thrust my feet into the river.

Fear, that's what was on my mind: fear of rapists, fear of bears, fear of loneliness, fear of getting lost, fear of being found (by mad rapists). And finally, the fear of being swallowed up by vast, empty wilderness.

While rapists and bears were high on the list, my greatest fear was getting lost. There was one part of the IAT that had me particularly worried: the Matane Reserve in Quebec. Before leaving for my hike, I'd called several people to ask about finding my way through this section. No one seemed to know much about it, but luckily my boyfriend had agreed to hike with me through there. With this reassuring thought, my fears soon drifted away. I looked around.

▲ *Bald eagle*

Too Thick to Drink, Not Quite Thick Enough to Walk On

Sunlight sparkled on waves in the river. Towering pines swayed gently in the wind. There wasn't a house, a road, a car in sight. But while this looked like untouched wilderness, it was anything but.

Like most of New England's major rivers, industrial and municipal waste was dumped into the Penobscot for most of the 20th century. The river was so polluted that the locals joked it was "too thick to drink, but not quite thick enough to walk on."

But despite years of abuse, the Penobscot is a lovely waterway. Approximately 560 kilometres in length, the river begins as the East and West branches in north-east Maine, wraps around Mount Katahdin, then empties into Penobscot Bay. Largely forested, the river valley is a refuge for an abundance of wildlife. Bald eagles, ospreys and great blue herons wheel above the flashing water, while white-tail deer wander along the banks. The river itself is crowded with brook trout, smallmouth bass, white perch and, most remarkably, wild Atlantic salmon.

In the early 1800s, approximately half a million Atlantic salmon returned to spawn in their native New England states each year. About 80,000 of these returned to the Penobscot River. Fish were so plentiful, they say, that fishermen could sit on their docks in deck chairs and catch them with dip nets.

The salmon run has declined in recent years, but the Penobscot River is still one of New England's richest salmon river.

Abelina

I soaked up the beauty for a while, then stood up, pulled my boots on and headed back to the road to face the mad rapists. A few seconds later, a car screeched to a stop beside me. The window whizzed down and a halo of white hair appeared.

"Hey, where ya headed?" quavered an old woman with twinkly eyes. Her face was a mass of wrinkles, except for two smooth spots in the middle of each cheek.

I told her I was headed for the campground a few miles away.

"Jump in. I'll take you to my place. You can camp out in the yard," she said.

More than anything, I wanted to jump in the car. The woman was wearing a hot pink blouse and looked like fun. But I couldn't. "I'm hiking the IAT," I explained. "I'm supposed to walk every step of the way."

"But I just live a few miles away," she said. "Hurry up, hurry up, jump in."

Rather than argue, I jumped in the car.

"My name is Abelina Gorham, I'm ninety-two years old, and I'm alone in the world," she said, simultaneously clearing off the front seat, thrusting out a gnarled hand and weaving down the road at breakneck speed.

We arrived at Abelina's house a few minutes later. Like her, everything in the house was ancient: the woven straw fly swatter in the bathroom, the wrought-iron chairs on the screened-in porch, the dusty-looking animal heads mounted throughout the house. Most perplexing was the worried-looking doe's head hanging above the dining room table.

Seeing me staring at the deer, Abelina explained that her cabin had once been a hunting camp. The animal trophies had come with the place when she and her husband, Earl, bought it in the 1960s.

Earl and Abelina lived in Connecticut, but came to Maine every summer. Then, in 1970, Abelina fell deathly ill. Told she had only three months to live, she begged Earl to let her die in their cabin in the woods.

Earl packed the car and drove Abelina to Maine. Abelina buried Earl fifteen years later. Having no desire to return to her native Connecticut, Abelina has lived here, all alone, for another fifteen years.

"I still miss Earl," Abelina said. "He was the love of my life, you know."

It was Abelina's mother, a person who "saw" things, who told her she'd marry him.

"Who's that?" her mother had whispered, pointing to a handsome young man across the church. Abelina was barely eighteen at the time.

"That's Earl Edmund Gorham," Abelina had whispered back.

"You'll be married to that boy in less that a year," her mother had said.

Abelina was shocked. She barely knew the boy. But, as predicted, the boy soon came courting in his 1927 Ford. In less than a year, she and Earl were married.

"He was quite the boy around town," Abelina confided, the note of triumph in her voice undiminished by time. Then, remembering he was gone, a dark shadow crossed her face.

She stood up and moved into the kitchen. Her steps were short and nervous, the gait of someone who suddenly felt every one of her ninety-two years. When she started rummaging in the cupboard, I leapt up and offered to cook up some of my hiking food. Abelina looked surprised, then gratefully tottered back to her chair.

Over steaming plates of instant noodles, I asked Abelina if she ever got scared living out here alone.

"Sure," she said. "A few times kids tried breaking in while I was asleep. That was scary, but I sleep with a big gun under my pillow."

I suddenly remembered how Abelina had picked me up on the road. She'd talked to me for all of thirty seconds before insisting that I go home with her. Abelina was spry for her age, but a gust of wind would blow her away. How did this frail old woman know that I wouldn't tie her to a chair and steal everything she owned?

Some of the many flowers that carpet the roadsides and meadows in northern Maine ▶

"You've got to trust people," she answered.

There was a certain irony here. I'm tall and young and strong, yet there I'd been, just a few hours ago, cowering from phantom rapists in the woods. Abelina is small and weak and old, yet she'd picked me up, a complete stranger, on a deserted country road.

After supper, Abelina insisted that I sleep on her screened-in porch that night. Streaks of gold were fading into the night sky as I crawled into my sleeping bag. I was relieved to be sleeping inside, as my intermittent cough had turned into a terrible cold. The sound of the Penobscot River, lapping over rocks in the distance, soon lulled me to sleep.

It was still dark when I waved goodbye to Abelina the next morning, a tiny bent figure waving from the porch. She looked terribly vulnerable, though I knew she was anything but. I walked to the end of the driveway, waved again, then headed north, feeling sad that I'd never see her again.

Mashed Potato Wrestling

The road wound its way through silent stands of trees. I walked quickly, buoyed by Abelina's kindness and a good night's sleep. The air was cool and sweet. Birds swung and chattered on the telephone wires. Dew glistened on clumps of wildflowers. A few hours later, I was striding through potato fields. The plants were covered in delicate white blossoms, so pretty that they say the fashionable Marie Antoinette once wove them through her hair.

They don't call Aroostook County "The Garden of Maine" for nothing. One of the few agriculturally productive regions in the state, the area is blanketed in a rich soil, called caribou loam. Broccoli, peas, hay and oats are big crops here, but it's the Maine potato that made this region famous.

Potatoes are Maine's most important agricultural commodity, and Aroostook County produces over 90 percent of them. Dozens of different varieties are grown here, so many that it's rumoured that specific potato crops are debated like vintages of fine wines.

One place you'll hear plenty of potato talk is at the Potato Blossom Festival in nearby Fort Fairfield. Munching on home-made potato chips, crowds of spectators jostle shoulders to watch the annual mashed potato wrestling event, the Maine potato recipe contest, and the coronation of the Maine Potato Queen. Unfortunately, I'd missed the festivities by just a few weeks.

I reached the Stacyville store by mid-afternoon. An abandoned building surrounded by tangled grass and wildflowers, it looked like a good place to stop for lunch. Peering through a broken window, I saw upturned chairs, a rusty wood stove and broken bottles strewn across the floor. Sheets of peeling wallpaper fluttered in the wind. When I tried opening the door, a vicious-looking cat streaked across the floor. I decided to skip lunch.

I was feeling blue when I reached the Sherman Mills junction, several hours later. There was something unsettling about spending so much time alone. I felt disconnected from everything I knew, like a bit of fluff floating on the wind. There was a roadside hamburger joint at the junction. To cheer myself up, I decided to treat myself to some onion rings. I wasn't really hungry, but the thought of hitting the road again was completely unappealing.

I worked my way through a plate of rings, leaving greasy thumbprints on the pages of my romance novel. When they were gone, I ordered an ice cream. When that was gone, I ordered a coffee. When that was gone, there was nothing left to do but pick up the pack, trudge down the driveway and head for Patten.

Abelina, Again!

Within minutes, a familiar car streaked by, then screeched to a stop in a spray of gravel. Abelina!

"Hey, jump in the car, I'm taking y'all to Patten!" Abelina said.

I was so happy to see her — ecstatic, in fact — but I couldn't go to Patten with her. My plan was to walk — not drive — the IAT. But Abelina had pinned up her hair, put on dangly earrings and driven for almost an hour to see me.

"I wanted to take you to Raymond's Clam Shack for supper," she said, her lower lip trembling.

I jumped in the car. We drove up a long hill, then stopped at a roadside pull-out so I could snap some pictures of Katahdin. Almost a hundred kilometres away, the mountain was now just a dark lump on the horizon. Except for a little help from Abelina, I'd walked all that way.

▲ *Broken glass and peeling paint at the abandoned Stacyville store near Sherman, Maine*

After supper at Raymond's, Abelina drove me over to Rodney Harris' place, a friend of hers from church. "Can this young lady sleep behind your barn?" Abelina asked. There were no campgrounds in Patten, so I wasn't sure what I'd do if he refused.

Harris, a retired potato farmer, was slow to respond. Not because he was opposed to the idea — he wasn't — but because he talks slower than anyone I've ever met.

"No problem at all," he said. Eventually.

The next morning, the grass behind Harris' barn was silver with dew when I zipped open the tent. I got up, packed my gear, then padded across the yard, leaving green footsteps in the shining grass. I stopped in to see Mr. Harris on my way downtown.

"How did y'all sleep?" he drawled, his fingers a blur of motion over a bit of metal clamped in a vise. Harris retired ten years ago, but he still rises at dawn and rattles around in the barn all day. Old habits die hard.

Harris had been a potato farmer for forty years. He'd enjoyed working the land. There was something biblical in the work: turning the soil, sowing the seeds, then feeding people with the fruits of his labour. Harris liked being his own boss, too. He felt like a free man knowing he could lock the barn door and go fishing whenever he wanted to. Not that he ever did.

Then Frito-Lay, his biggest customer, started trying to tell this mild-mannered man how to run his farm. "They tried tellin' me what to plant and when," said Harris. "Got to feeling like it wasn't my farm anymore, so I quit."

Judging from Harris' barn (spotless), his lawn (perfectly clipped) and his house (freshly repainted), adapting to retirement was an ongoing challenge. Leaving Harris pacing like a restless bull in his barn, I went downtown in search of breakfast.

Patten had a few restaurants to choose from, but I chose the one with the frilly blue curtains, figuring that wherever there were frilly curtains, apple-cheeked grannies and home-made biscuits couldn't be far behind.

The bustling restaurant was bright and cheerful, so I sat down and ordered breakfast. While I was waiting for my food to arrive, an old man came in, sat down and asked for a cup of coffee.

Two kids, who'd been colouring on their placemats, ran over when they saw him. "Lloyd, Lloyd," they giggled, climbing up on his knees. A smile brightened the old man's face. A few minutes later, a young man swaggered in. A thick tree of a boy, his face was burnt red by the sun. "Lloyd, how are you?" he said, his voice quiet and respectful.

In cities, old men like Lloyd linger in malls and coffee shops, but who they are and how they got there mean nothing to anyone. Here in Patten, that old man seemed like someone to just about everyone.

Dodging Logging Trucks on Route 11

After breakfast, I headed north up Route 11. According to a roadside information sign, this was just a rough track through the woods in the 1800s, so narrow that "the sun has but little effect on it," and so treacherous it was "little else but a deep pit of mire." Today, Route 11 is a pretty country road dotted with farmhouses, each with a car-chasing dog out front. It would have been a pleasant four-hour walk to the Moro Road except for one thing: the logging trucks. Air brakes squealing, logs flailing, wood chips flying, they roared past every few minutes like demons possessed.

Many of those trucks likely belonged to J. D. Irving, one of the largest timber companies in the region. This company owns about 600,000 hectares of land in Maine, including much of the land along the proposed route of the IAT between Baxter Park and Mars Hill. So far, Irving has shown limited interest in the IAT project. Like other large industrial landowners in the area, they're worried that their right to cross the path might be jeopardised, or that "shadow zoning" might restrict or eliminate timber cutting well beyond the trail corridor.

Today, only thirty of the 260 kilometres of the IAT in Maine are actually in the woods. Most of these trails are near Mars Hill, where several small landowners have agreed to allow hikers access to their land. It may take years to gain the support of powerful landowners like Irving, but IAT founder Dick Anderson remains optimistic.

"We'll wait. Heck, if it takes twenty-five years, we'll wait," Anderson said. "Gaining the support of landowners takes time. Just look at the Appalachian Trail. It took them seventy-five years to get their trail off the roads and into the woods."

The Moro Road

I got to the Moro Road junction at five o'clock. It was too early to camp, so I headed east down the deserted country road.

After dodging logging trucks on Route 11 all day, the silence on the Moro Road was blissful. A few hours passed, then I started looking for a place to camp. There wasn't a campsite for miles. I walked down the road scanning the bushes in the fading light, trying to decide what to do. Finally, I just headed into an overgrown field, thrashed around in the waist-high grass to flatten it down, then set up my tent and crawled into bed. Too tired to eat, I watched the sunset through the swaying grass and fell asleep.

The next morning, a heavy fog hung over the field and the grass was dripping with dew. Walking over to where I'd stashed my gear under a tree, I was soon soaked to the skin. Shivering and coughing, I tried lighting the stove. It still wouldn't start, so I packed everything up, sloshed down to the road and began walking again. My plan was to stop at the first likely looking farmhouse, linger hopefully near their coffee pot, and wait for the mist to clear.

The fog was so thick, I could barely see the pavement. A farmhouse soon appeared on the left, a gaunt shadow in the mist. When I got closer, I saw that the paint was peeling and there were ripped curtains hanging at the windows. There were two cars in the yard, but one was sagging on a jack and the other was flipped over on its hood. I abandoned the notion of coffee.

The fog lifted like a theatre curtain when the sun came out a few hours later. Tired, hungry and drenched in sweat, I was truly ready for a break when I reached the end of the Moro Road. From here, the IAT would follow Route 2 to Houlton, about twenty-five kilometres away. But first, I needed a nap.

I stepped off the road, dropped my pack and collapsed in the tall grass. The air smelled faintly of honey. Wind whispered through the grass. Sunlight lay in patches on my tummy. The heat and sun dragged at my eyelids, and I soon fell asleep.

A logging truck roared by, jolting me awake. I fell asleep. A few minutes later, another logging truck went by. After the third truck, I stood up in disgust. So far on this trip, I'd seen more trees on the back of logging trucks than I had in the woods.

Johnny Down Under

After my nap, I started walking again. A few kilometres down the road, a man was pulling out of his driveway just as I was walking by. He braked when he saw me, blocking my passage down the road.

"Hey — where ya going?" he slurred. "Wanna beer?"

"Uh, no thanks. Just had lunch," I said primly, glancing into the battered car as I walked by. A man in his late forties, he had bloodshot eyes and a beer can wedged between his legs. He wore a greasy cap that said "Vietnam Vet — and proud of it."

This was it! My mad rapist!! (Although in the full-fledged version of my nightmare, there were usually four wild-eyed rapists in the car).

"Well, how about some sun tea up at the trailer then?" he said. "The wife's up there. Stuck on the couch with a bad back. She'd love a visitor."

It took him fifteen minutes to coax me up the driveway. By the time he'd stepped out of the car and lurched up the stairs to the trailer, I'd made my decision. He was drunk and he wasn't very big. I could take him out if I had to. Besides, I was curious about the sun tea.

"You'd better have a wife in there," I said, dropping my pack.

There was a wife in the trailer. A sweet-faced woman in her mid-forties, Debbie was lying on the sofa doing needlepoint. And the sun tea — twelve tea bags in a pitcher of water steeped in the sun for the afternoon — was

▲ John Camilleri (nicknamed "Johnny Down Under" because he lives in a cave), standing in his garden near Ludlow, Maine

delicious. I was finishing my third glass when Dave said "Hey — let's have a barbecue tonight." They talked it over, called their neighbour Connie, then Dave went to pick up Johnny Down Under, the guy he was on his way to visit when I met him on the road.

◄ Waking up in a mist-shrouded field on the Moro Road

Johnny Down Under is the local hermit. A wiry little man with a long, tumbling beard, Johnny Down Under lives in a cave nearby. Something had happened in Johnny's life a few years back. A family tragedy was Debbie's guess, but she didn't know for sure. Whatever it was made Johnny move to this remote corner of Maine and shun the trappings of modern life.

Johnny lives in a cave without running water or electricity. His days are spent chasing butterflies, watching his garden grow and reading very difficult books. Johnny lives alone. He's shared his cave with a few girlfriends, but eventually they always want to improve the place, and that's when the problems begin.

At the barbecue, Johnny Down Under told me a story.

Johnny had a friend, Big Bill. In America, everyone has a nickname. Big Bill's nickname fits: he's six and a half feet tall and wide as a barn door.

One day Big Bill invited Johnny Down Under for supper. It was November 1999, a few weeks before the dawn of the new millennium. Over supper, Johnny and Bill got to talking about Y2K. The conversation became quite animated. Bill pulled out a bible and began reading from Revelations. Johnny bowed his head and listened carefully, as is his way.

Then Big Bill picked up a framing hammer and whacked Johnny on the head. Johnny's skull cracked open. Johnny went down. Then Big Bill took a pair of vice grips and broke Johnny's fingers one by one. Then he picked up Johnny's limp body, slung it over his shoulder and climbed the stairs to the second floor. Then he flung Johnny's body out of the bedroom window.

After Johnny told me that story, I stopped being scared of mad rapists. What was the point? It's never what you fear that'll get you — what'll get you is something you could never expect. This was a lesson I was to learn again and again on my IAT hike.

After eight months of convalescence, Johnny was fine, if a little spooked. They hauled Big Bill off to the lunatic asylum where he still is to this day.

Discussing Gun Control with a Fiercely Patriotic, Well-lubed American

Back at the barbecue, the pile of empty beer cans grew as the evening progressed. Then the conversation turned to gun control. Now, if there's one subject you shouldn't discuss with a fiercely patriotic, well-lubed American, it's gun control. Suddenly Dave and I were shouting at each other.

"What about the Montreal Massacre?" I yelled. "Some crazy nut went into a Montreal university with a gun and murdered fourteen women. Several more were wounded."

"Guns aren't bad, people are bad," Dave shot back.

"Yeah, but if you took all the guns away, those bad people couldn't shoot people," I said.

"You can never take all the guns away," Dave snapped.

We glowered at each other over the crackling fire.

"More potato salad anyone?" asked Debbie.

The bowl was passed around, fresh beers were cracked and the conversation wandered off. I left the party soon after, though I made sure to whack Dave on the back a few times and laugh extra hard at his jokes before leaving.

I wasn't angry with Dave after our conversation. Quite the opposite, in fact. Snuggling into my sleeping bag, I fell asleep thinking I'd learned something fundamental about Americans. On the issue of gun control, I'd assumed that all rational people thought like me: that guns were for policemen, not civilians. Given this power, our policemen then protect us. Yet Dave and Debbie had two guns. Connie, their neighbour, had five (a widow living alone, she fears for her safety). Even little Abelina had a gun.

These were all rational people, yet they all owned guns. For them, it wasn't enough to rely on policemen for protection. First, they needed to be able to rely on themselves. In America, that often means buying a gun. And there was no way someone like me — a grubby Canadian backpacker — was going to talk them out of it.

As I was packing up to leave the next day, Connie came over and slipped a small plastic container into my hand.

"I'd feel much better about your safety if you carried this," she said. "It's illegal in Canada, so mail it back when you get to the border."

It was mace. America was growing more alarming by the moment. I'd never seen mace before. It belonged in that hazy category that included muggings, darkened alleys and graffiti-covered subway trains. Thanking Connie, I slid the dispenser into my pocket. It was only about the size of a cigarette lighter, but it felt like a

"Seed and Table Potatoes." Buildings like this are a common sight near Monticello, Maine, where the IAT wends its way through rolling potato fields. ▶

loaf of bread banging against my leg as I walked down the driveway, then headed east down Route 2.

Musing About Mules

On my way to Houlton, I stopped in at Johnny Down Under's cave. He gave me a tour of the garden. Dancing ahead like a mayfly, he ripped a head of lettuce from the earth. It tasted of hope. He captured a damselfly in his leathery palm and showed me its gossamer wings. He showed me where the moose came, every evening, to the pond at the bottom of the garden.

A few hours later, Johnny walked me to Houlton. He was still weak from the beating Big Bill had given him, but gamely offered to carry my pack.

"Gawd, that thing's heavy," he said, handing it back a half hour later. We swapped the pack back and forth until a few kilometres outside Houlton, where we stopped at an outdoor supply store.

While repairing my stove, the owner tried to sell me a mule.

"Why carry that dratted thing when my mule could do it for you?" he said, jabbing his thumb towards my backpack. This wasn't a good idea, but I couldn't say why. I pictured floating down the trail, the mule plodding along behind me with my pack. I pictured stroking the animal's neck while surveying a mountainous vista. When I pictured myself sitting by a crackling campfire, the mule grazing contentedly in the darkness, I knew it was time to leave.

Johnny Down Under walked me all the way to a campsite outside Houlton. We said goodbye, then I watched him walk back up the road, a light skipping figure, bending to poke at things by the side of the road, then continuing on again.

From Rails to Trails

After Houlton, the designated IAT route follows a confusing maze of secondary roads to Mars Hill. None of these roads appeared on my map. Rather than wandering aimlessly down unmarked gravel roads, I opted to follow the abandoned Bangor and Aroostook Trail from Houlton to Mars Hill.

Until the 1950s, the Bangor and Aroostook Railroad carried 60,000 carloads of potatoes out of this region every year. Then, thanks to the decline of Maine's potato industry and the new interstate that was built nearby, the railway fell into disuse. The weedy eyesore was eventually leased to the state of Maine, who pulled up the tracks and built a recreational trail.

The B&A Trail was calm and peaceful. Trees swayed in the wind, birds flitted through the air and the evil road was far, far away. I didn't see a soul until just outside Bridgewater, when I met two women out for an evening stroll. One of them offered me the use of her backyard that night. She came by to chat as I was setting up my tent.

"Bridgewater is the nicest little town in the world," she said. When the sun set that night, dousing the houses across the valley in liquid copper, I had to agree.

The next day, I followed the B&A Trail out of Bridgewater and headed towards Mars Hill. I stopped, midway, in the village of Robinsons.

Robinsons is the kind of place you remember living in as a child, even if you never did. There was a pond in the centre of the village, colourful houses were scattered across the hillsides, and the air smelled of freshly cut grass and wet laundry drying in the sun.

Coming into the village, I passed two trucks parked in the middle of the main road. Chatting through their open windows, one driver watched a gang of kids playing a lazy game of stick hockey while the other squinted up at the cloudless sky. I strolled down to the pond, threw my pack down and sprawled out on the grass. Robinsons was so pleasant, I'd probably be there still if it weren't for the IAT.

Border Bound

After Robinsons, I followed the trail into Mars Hill. After a quick lunch at a greasy diner, I walked through town and headed up Mars Hill Mountain. It was a hard, steep climb, but the view from the top was well worth the effort. There was an IAT shelter up there, but it was too early to stop for the night. Besides, I was eager to reach the Canada/U.S. border.

On top of Mars Hill, the IAT trail followed a road along the summit, then plunged into the forest. After the road, the woods felt close and claustrophobic. Strange noises erupted in the distance. It started getting dark. A deep instinctive

▲ *The Bangor and Aroostook rail/trail near Bridgewater, Maine*

fear flooded my body: must-be-home-by-dark-or-disaster-will-strike. I got lost, panicked, found the trail again, then a few minutes later, burst out of the woods into a farmer's field.

The sun lay, soft and golden, on the field of swaying grain. I waded through the field down to the road, turned right and walked the short distance to the border. On the other side of the fence, I saw a Canadian house with Canadian smoke puffing out the chimney. There was a Canadian dog tied to the porch. It thumped its Canadian tail when I whistled.

I would spend the next few days walking along the border, so I wasn't home yet. But I was happy — so very happy — to be only a stone's throw away.

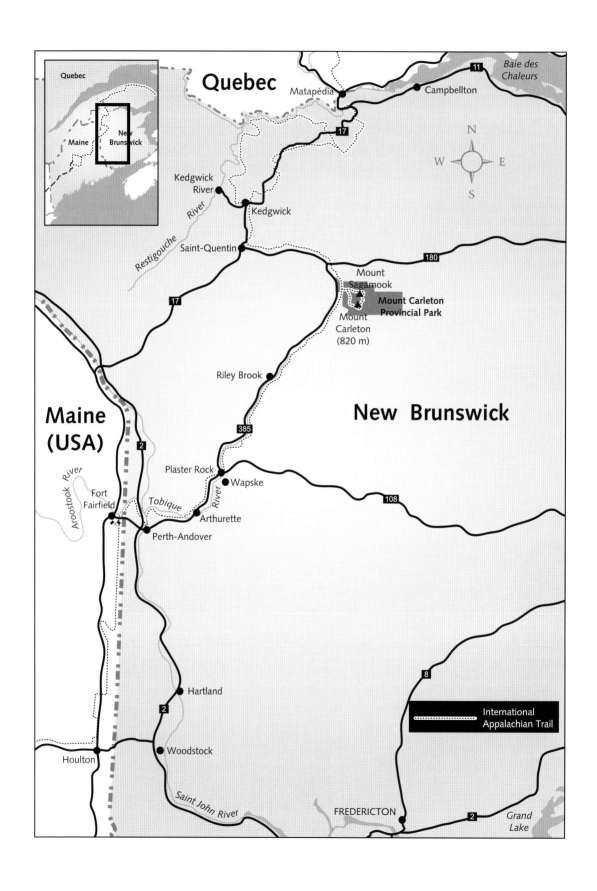

Section Two

NEW BRUNSWICK

Profound Boredom

I camped close to the border that night. Once the tent was up, I cooked some instant noodles and ate them straight from the pot. I ate slowly because once I was finished, I had nothing to do: it was too early for bed and I'd finished all my romance novels.

After supper, I washed my pot and spoon. That killed forty-five seconds. I lay on my back and watched a caterpillar crawl up a blade of grass. That killed another two minutes. I stood up and looked around. There was nothing to see but swaying grass in every direction.

What was wrong with me? Why was I so bored? After weeks of walking, I was expecting an epiphany, a flash of insight, a peek into the belly button of the divine. In *Walking the Appalachian Trail*, author Larry Luxenberg explains that after a long period of hiking:

> You can expect to undergo some personality changes. A heightened affinity for nature infiltrates your life. Greater inner peace. Enhanced self-esteem ... more appreciation for what you have and less desire to acquire what

53

you don't. A childlike zest for living life to the fullest. A refusal to be embarrassed about having fun. (P. 271)

So far, I felt exactly the same. I went to bed feeling like a failure.

The stars were as thick as snowflakes when I got up for a late night nature's call. When I got back to the tent, I tried standing, Thoreau-like, in the middle of the field. Bugs chewed my ankles. Sleep dragged at my eyelids. I lasted fifteen seconds. Crawling into my still-warm sleeping bag, I made a policy decision: I was going to leave the profound thinking to others.

The next morning, I headed north up the Canada/U.S. border.

Toeing the Line

The international boundary is a narrow band of no-man's-land between Canada and the United States. Since the border runs right up the middle of the strip, IAT hikers can walk with one foot in either country — a philosophical point that trail founder Dick Anderson thinks is important.

▲ *A bilingual IAT sign on the international boundary near Fort Fairfield, Maine*

"I wanted people to think philosophically about the concept of borders," he said. "Nothing respects them but us. Forests blow seeds from one side to the other, and clouds and butterflies fly back and forth. The idea was to get people thinking about the earth as a whole."

The IAT runs along the border from Mars Hill, Maine, to the Fort Fairfield border crossing, a brisk one-day walk. It was a relief being on a trail after days of road walking. Raspberry bushes lined both sides of the trail. I stopped often, scooping handfuls of damp berries into my mouth.

The trail was easy at first, then it dipped down through a series of swamps. Grassy humps poked out of pools of stagnant water. I hopped from hump to hump, trying to escape wet feet, but inevitably, I missed my step and sank to my knees with a watery plop. I pulled myself out by grabbing onto a nearby spruce tree, then started walking again.

The trail got worse and worse. After a few hours of slogging, I saw a road heading off to the left. I decided to leave the trail and take the road the rest of the way to Fort Fairfield. I was sure it was close by.

It wasn't. I passed men hovering over smoky barbecues, kids playing beside a lake, bored dogs barking at the end of their chains. Finally, I was too tired to take another step. I dropped my pack, slipped my boots off and collapsed in the ditch.

Just then, a young couple walked by on the opposite side of the road. When they spotted me, I pretended to be tying my shoe, not lying in the ditch. I leapt to my feet when they approached.

"Hey, how are you, where ya headed?" said the man, a tall, blond creature with golden skin. His wife, also blonde, was equally stunning. Beside them, I felt like a smelly old shoe. Plus, I was so tired I could barely stand.

"Oh, up the road," I said vaguely, hoping they'd go away.

Their flawless faces fell. Feeling guilty, I forced out a few complete sentences. They invited me to their house to fill my canteen. I wasn't thirsty, but it seemed rude to refuse.

When we arrived at the house, a crowd of men were eating supper on the porch. Friends and neighbours from both sides of the border, they get together every year to help with the harvest.

The men sat, chairs tipped against the house, trading one-liners between sips of beer and bites of food. Excited children chased each other through the crowd. A woman circulated with a plate of hot brownies. Two dogs rolled around in the driveway, growling playfully. The scene, bathed in the late afternoon sun, looked like a Norman Rockwell painting sprung to life.

Someone handed me a plate of lasagne. Someone else handed me a beer. A homemade brownie landed on my plate. Suddenly, a tear plopped onto my plate. Lowering my head, I glared at my food, willing myself not to cry.

I was overflowing with gratitude for the careless generosity extended by these strangers. A plate of food, a beer, a few kind words — it meant nothing to them. But for me, these gifts were priceless. I felt part of the human race again. Travelling alone, I hadn't realized how isolated I'd felt.

I managed to get through supper without bursting into tears, then picked up my backpack and fled. When I looked back, everyone was standing at the end of the driveway, waving goodbye.

The Offending Backpack

A few kilometres down the road, I came to the Fort Fairfield border crossing. I snapped a photo of the U.S. customs building, walked across the border, then snapped a photo of the Canadian customs building.

Then I turned to take one last look at America. Silhouetted against the setting sun, the U.S. customs building looked spectacular, so I left my backpack, walked back across the border and snapped one last photo.

A Canadian customs official suddenly appeared.

"It is illegal to enter Canada, then cross back into the States while leaving personal effects on the Canadian side," she said, buzzing around me like an angry bee. My offending backpack, propped against a lamp post, was exactly five metres away.

Walking along the international boundary, I'd been criss-crossing between Canada and America all day. When I pointed this out to the border guard, she growled alarmingly and stomped away.

I picked up my pack with a weary sigh, then followed an eighteen-wheeler to the customs building.

The window was so high, I could barely see over the sill. This forced me to look up at the customs official like an errant child. Glaring down, the woman ran through the usual list of questions.

"Yes, I do have a gun. A sawed-off shotgun, in fact," I wanted to answer, but didn't. "I'm also carrying a case of whiskey and four cartons of cigarettes. Everything's right here in my backpack."

Moments later, I was through customs and standing on Canadian soil. Despite the cranky customs official, it was great to be home again.

I camped near the customs building that night. After setting up the tent, I scanned the New Brunswick trail guide. Ahead, the IAT ran along the border for a few more kilometres, then turned east and followed a converted rail/trail for several days.

Setting off the next morning, I immediately encountered a huge beaver dam. Skirting the edge, I hopped across a swamp, then waded through a sea of waist-high grass. The grass was dripping wet but smelled sweetly of starflowers, wood sorrel and wild lily-of-the-valley. I sloshed through the flowers, then followed the trail up a hill. From the top, I could see the Aroostook River far below, and beside it, the Tinker Line Railway.

The Tinker Line is part of a 2,000-kilometre network of abandoned railway beds converted into recreational trails called the New Brunswick Trail System. The IAT would follow this trail system until Plaster Rock, about fifty kilometres away.

The Tinker Line was a narrow gravel path, winding through the trees. Miniature road signs dotted the trailside, telling hikers when to keep right, veer left and stop. The trail followed the Aroostook River for a few kilometres, then turned north and followed the Saint John River.

The Rhine of America

Dubbed "the Rhine of America" by homesick European settlers, the Saint John starts as a blue trickle in northern Maine, forms the international boundary for 130 kilometres, meanders south-east across New Brunswick, then empties into the Bay of Fundy, a distance of 673 kilometres.

There's an old story about the Saint John River region. It may even be true. But truth or fiction, the tale captures the essence of New Brunswick's most important waterway.

Up a tributary of the Saint John River in the early 1900s, woodsmen began dressing in the latest British fashions: starched wing collars, boiled shirts, white gloves and shiny patent leather shoes. The woodsmen were given these clothes by an Englishman who was living in their midst.

Every year, the Englishman's family sent him clothes made by exclusive British tailors and haberdashers, and every year, he passed these packages on to his friends. The Englishman — who lived in a shack and wore nothing but work clothes — had no use for finery.

"One lives like a gentleman here," he explained. "One has all the fishing and shooting one wants at one's door. This is a happy land."

▲ *Black bear*

As I walked beside it, the Saint John River did indeed seem charmed. The rain had stopped, leaving plumes of mist hanging above the river, and the air smelled warm and earthy, like rotting autumn leaves.

The trail followed the river for a while, then veered off into a gravel pit. Giving a wide berth to the heavy machinery, I descended into a steep valley, scrambled up a grease-spattered slope, then picked up the trail again. A few miles further, and I was in Perth-Andover.

Bear-infested Wilderness

Before Perth-Andover was settled in the early 1800s, there were only a few fur traders, a handful of Acadians and several bands of Algonquin Indians living in New Brunswick. Then waves of Irish started to arrive. Some Scots turned up. A band of Danes wandered through. Some Germans, some Loyalists and some Jews came too. But mostly, the newcomers were Irish.

The early 1800s were a difficult time in Ireland. Poorhouses were bursting, mother-less orphans wandered the streets, and endless lines of dull-eyed people shuffled through soup kitchens. Waves of immigrants began leaving the country due to poor economic conditions. Millions more fled during the Great Irish Potato Famine of 1845–50; roughly half the population emigrated.

▲ *A farmers' cemetery in the middle of a potato field near Arthurette, New Brunswick*

Many boarded ships and headed for America. Watching Ireland's lush shores recede in the distance, they probably thought the worst was behind them. They were wrong: the immigrant ships were little more than floating coffins. Living conditions were appalling, food was scarce, and cholera and typhus ran rampant. Thousands died en route. Most times, corpses were tossed overboard. One woman, however, was unable to throw her dead child into the Atlantic. Instead, she salted down the tiny corpse, stored it in a trunk, and stepped ashore with the makeshift coffin under her arm.

Many of the Irish who arrived in New Brunswick didn't stay long. For them, the province was just a stepping-stone to the United States. Passage to Canada was cheaper than America, and Canada didn't charge an immigrant tax at the time.

Those with money left immediately. Others stayed just long enough to earn their passage. Many simply picked up their suitcases and started walking. Only the poorest and least fit stayed behind in New Brunswick.

Imagine watching friends and family die around you, imagine being forced to flee your ancestral homeland, imagine surviving the coffin ships, then imagine arriving — poorly clothed, flat broke and emotionally exhausted — in New Brunswick.

We're not talking sandy beaches, coconuts and soft, tropical breezes here. We're talking frigid temperatures, frontier living and vast tracks of bear-infested wilderness. We were "like children abandoned in the merciless woods," one settler said, describing his arrival in the Perth-Andover region.

Today, a patchwork of farmers' fields has replaced the dense forest, and Perth-Andover has become a bustling village of nearly 2,000 people.

Stealth Camping

I stopped at a gas station to ask for directions to the nearest campground. When I learned that it was several kilometres away, I decided to stealth camp in downtown Perth-Andover that night.

I wandered through the drowsy, suburban streets, looking for a place to camp. Then I passed a white bungalow. The building had no windows, and only one door. Beside the door was a small red sign: "Contact fire chief if building burns down." Whatever this building was, it didn't look residential. I looked left and right. No one was around, so I dashed behind the building.

Behind the building was a searchlight, a garbage bin and a large fan protruding from the back wall. I opened the garbage can. There were wire clippings inside. Then the fan switched on. It ran for exactly one minute, then quit. Ten minutes later, it ran again, then stopped. It was all very odd, but I decided to camp there that night.

I set up my tent behind the house, hung some wet laundry on the garbage can, cooked up a pot of beans under the fan (which continued to switch on and off relentlessly), then crawled into my sleeping bag.

That night, I had a dream. I was writing a story about a woman who was camped behind a white bungalow, when a flashlight suddenly shone down on my page. Looking up, I saw the black knee-high boots of a police officer, who arrested me for writing a story about a woman who was camped beside a white bungalow, when a flashlight suddenly shone down on my ...

Then I heard a scream, right outside my tent.

I woke up, shot out of bed and stood there — eyes bulging and teeth chattering — under the searchlight. Then two cats streaked out of the bushes, hissing and yowling as they ran.

Suddenly I was hunched over, laughing, in the weirdest campsite on the IAT. This was not the wilderness experience I'd imagined when I set off two weeks ago.

The Tobique River

It was raining when I left Perth-Andover the next day. The railway followed the Saint John River for a few kilometres, then turned east and headed up the Tobique River.

The Tobique captured my heart from the moment I saw it. Except for the plop of raindrops falling from the trees, it was completely silent. Mist rose off the clear, green water, and fingers of sunlight poked through the swirling clouds. I was only a few kilometres from Perth-Andover, but it felt as if I'd arrived somewhere sacred and untouched.

I walked a bit farther, then passed a dam. Built in 1951, the Tobique Hydroelectric Dam was constructed on land owned by the Tobique Nation Indian Reserve. Before the dam, the river was a place of power and grandeur, where bold young men shot the rapids in birch-bark canoes.

Today, the dam spans the river like an unwieldy set of orthodontic braces, and this once-swift river has slowed to a trickle. Though beautiful still, the Tobique seems desolate today. It cries out for the silken swoosh of canoes, the rain of droplets falling from lifted paddles, the echo of boyish voices bouncing off the rocks.

Before the dam, the Tobique was one of the richest salmon rivers in North

Floating down the Tobique River in a hand-made Miller canoe ▶

America — so rich that influential people from the United States and Europe travelled here to fish in the early 1900s. Exclusive fishing lodges sprang up; the Rockefellers, the Roosevelts and the Duke and Duchess of Windsor once fished here. Fishing clubs were formed. And membership wasn't cheap: in 1908, one member paid $4,000 to join the Tobique Salmon Club. Locals were drafted into service as outfitters, guides and camp cooks. Most were happy to oblige, as the outsiders brought money — and plenty of it — into this impoverished region.

There was only one problem. In addition to building fishing lodges, the outsiders were also snapping up much of the choicest land along the Tobique. Soon they controlled most of the fishing rights, which made it illegal for the locals to fish in their own river. The residents weren't pleased about this, but there was little they could do.

"So everyone became expert poachers," Bill Miller, a Nictau canoe-builder, explained to me. "The warden, who was a local, would tell everyone when he was goin' to Riley Brook — and he'd say it real clear: 'I'm-goin'-to-Riley-Brook,' so everyone knew it was safe to fish everywhere else but there. When the warden got back, he'd get plenty of supper invitations. Fresh salmon was usually on the menu."

Ironically, fishing rights are no longer an issue on the Tobique River. Since the dam went in, salmon stocks have become so depleted that fishing is prohibited today.

Bliss in the Railroader's Hut

A bolt of lightning split the sky as I walked past the dam. Thunder cracked a few seconds later, then rain began to fall in torrents. When a bolt of lightning struck the trail a few hundred metres ahead, I decided to dodge beneath a tree for cover.

I huddled there, head buried in my arms, as the thunderstorm grew in fury. The rain fell harder and harder. Rivulets of water began creeping beneath the tree. I reached out to yank the pack in. That's when I spotted a dark blob across the trail. I fished out a scarf and dried off my glasses.

There was a deserted railroader's hut, right across the trail!

The hut was about two metres square. There was no door and the floor was covered with broken glass, but miraculously, it was dry. I dashed inside, stripped off my wet clothes and lit the stove. Within minutes, I was curled in my sleeping bag, a cup of hot cocoa in hand, watching the storm from the doorway.

"This is life stripped down to basics: warmth, shelter and hot chocolate," I thought, my eyelids drifting closed. "What bliss."

It was still raining when I woke up the next morning. I put my wet clothes back on, ate a quick breakfast and hit the trail.

I decided to try for Plaster Rock that day, twenty-five kilometres away. As a reward for getting through another rainy day, I decided I would stay in a hotel. I pictured lying on a soft bed, watching gangster movies on TV. I'd have a hot bath, and order room service, and talk on the phone and ...

Fighting Bears with Silver Bells

It was a long, wet day. The railway bed was easy walking, but there wasn't much to see. Then, late afternoon, I passed a yellow sign: "Settler's Inn, Plaster Rock, 5 km."

I was walking about four kilometres an hour. If I walked a bit faster, I could be there in an hour.

I picked up the pace. Soon I spotted another yellow sign in the distance. A burst of hot joy flooded through my veins. The sign was too far away to read, but I was sure it would say: "Settler's Inn: 500 metres."

It said: "Settler's Inn: 4 km." I picked up a rock and flung it at the sign. I considered stopping for the night, but images of soft beds floated in the air.

I started walking again. Then, trudging past a row of mist-shrouded trees, I heard a twig snap. Then I heard CRASH! THUD! CRASH!

I couldn't see it, but I knew it was a bear. Pawing frantically for my bear bell, I cursed every one of Montreal's outdoor stores: I didn't have any bear spray.

"All sold out," they'd said. But I'd gone looking for bear spray during a truly Canadian news week. That week, a camper in British Columbia had been attacked by a wolf, while a few days earlier, a young Olympic hopeful had been killed by a black bear. It didn't matter that fatal black bear attacks are practically unheard of in Quebec — that week, Montreal's outdoor stores had been mobbed by terrified campers searching for bear spray.

Bear spray is atomized capsicum — hot pepper dust in a spray can. It comes with a "quick draw holster," and can blast bears up to six metres away. Studies have

shown that bear spray is more effective than firearms: an 85 percent success rate compared to 50 percent for guns. Pepper spray also protects bears, as it's non-toxic.

Bear spray is a good thing, but I didn't have any. This left me facing a bear on a deserted trail with a tiny silver bell in my hand.

In his book *Bear Attacks, Their Causes and Avoidance*, author Stephen Herrero lovingly reviews every bear attack in North America between 1900 and 1980. Herrero's findings are surprising: in all that time, only twenty-three people were killed by black bears. Considering there are half a million black bears in North America, Herrero concluded that "black bears [rarely] use their power to injure or kill people."

Herrero had researched his topic extensively, but he'd missed one crucial area of study: the survival rate of bell-ringing hikers.

I rang the bell. Silence. Then a tiny bear cub darted across the trail a short distance ahead. Then I heard a THUD! in the bushes beside me.

Stumbling across one bear is bad. Seeing two bears is worse. Finding yourself trapped between a mama bear and a baby bear is about as bad as it gets.

I turned around and ran: back down the trail, back past the Settler's Inn sign, back past a rock where I'd taken a rest. Then I stopped. Backtracking didn't make sense. No matter how far I went, I'd have to pass the bears eventually.

I turned around and went back up the trail, yelling and clapping my hands as I ran. I passed the place where I'd seen the bear cub, then burned up two more kilometres of trail. I stopped, wheezing madly, beside another yellow sign.

It said "Settler's Inn: 3 km." I cursed, shook my fist at the rainy heavens, then started plodding again.

An hour later, I saw the lights of Plaster Rock through the trees. Then the trail left the forest, followed the road for a while and crossed a bridge over the Tobique River. When I was halfway across the bridge, a procession of logging trucks lumbered by, making the bridge sway underfoot. Gripping the handrail, I inched my way across the bridge, then climbed the long hill towards town.

"... But That Includes Access to the Swimming Pool!"

There was an Irving Gas Station and store at the top of the hill. Lit by powerful spotlights, it looked like Noah's Ark tossing on a sea of brooding clouds. I staggered

◀ *Lush glade in New Brunswick's Mount Carleton Provincial Park* up to the building, dropped my pack and went inside.

The sudden heat made my glasses steam up. After wiping them off, I was greeted by a vision of gleaming pop bottles, shiny chocolate bars and a row of steaming coffee pots. I squished over to the coffee, poured myself a cup of the oily-looking brew, then sloshed to the bank machine at the back of the store. After withdrawing my last $70, I paid for my coffee and crossed the street to Settler's Inn.

"It's $78 for the night," the desk clerk said. I must have looked disappointed, because he added, "But that includes free parking and access to the swimming pool!"

I muttered something about their crappy signs, whirled around and stomped out the door. There was a campground right next door. Except for one damp-looking tent, the place was deserted. I carefully examined each campsite, then chose a dripping wet spot under a pine tree.

I pulled my tent out: it was wet. I pulled my sleeping bag out: it was wet. I pulled my sleeping mattress out: it was wet. I pulled my towel out: it was dry! I left everything in a sodden heap and headed for the showers.

I slept until noon the next day. Opening my eyes, I had to blink a few times. The tent was bathed with clear orange light, and steam rose off my sleeping bag. Could it be? When I zipped the tent open, I saw that it was: sun! And not a cloud in sight. I got up and went over to the Irving Station for a coffee.

Irvingland

They don't call New Brunswick "Irvingland" for nothing.

At the age when other boys were playing marbles and catching frogs, young Kenneth Colin Irving was standing behind the counter of his father's general store. Then, at the age when his friends stopped stealing apples and started chasing girls, K.C. Irving opened his first gas station in Bouctouche, New Brunswick. The year was 1924. K.C. Irving was twenty-five years old.

Over the course of his lifetime, Irving would build up an empire that included hundreds of gas stations, timberland, pulp and paper mills, shipyards, an oil refinery, building supply stores, newspapers, radio stations and — heck why not — a few french fry plants.

Cut a tree on Irving land, and it's likely brought to an Irving mill by an Irving truck — which is probably running on Irving gas and driven by an Irving truck driver.

En route to the mill, the Irving truck driver might stop at an Irving restaurant. Sipping a cup of Irving coffee while browsing through a Irving newspaper, he might like to order some Irving fries, even though his wife — a clerk at an Irving hardware store — had been making wisecracks about his waistline.

Getting up to leave, the driver might wipe his lips on an Irving napkin, leave a tip for the Irving waitress, then saunter back to his truck whistling a tune he'd heard on an Irving radio station.

It's no wonder that K.C. Irving was one of the world's richest men when he died in 1993. Today, Irving's three sons run the family business. These men, now in their seventies, are worth an estimated five billion dollars.

"And them's no small potatoes," as they say in these parts.

The Hour Between the Dog and the Wolf

A man in greasy coveralls was entering the Irving store just as I was walking up. He gallantly held the door open, then elbowed his way through the crowd of men loitering near the coffee urns.

"Hey boys, how 'bout dat ting up dere, shinin' in the sky!" he said, pouring himself a cup.

"How in the heck are you doin, George?" replied a man with work-cracked hands. "Havin' a little coffee with your sugar, I see," he joked, watching the newcomer rip open a handful of sugar packets and dump them into his coffee.

A companionable silence descended.

"Been a piss poor summer so far," commented a man wearing a carpenter's belt.

"Yep," replied another.

"You got 'er," said the talkative one.

"Mmmmm," offered the last one, who probably hasn't uttered a full sentence in years.

I overheard all this while loitering in the baked goods aisle. I desperately wanted a coffee, but the wall of grunting manliness around the coffee pots made me feel girlish and shy — which was ridiculous, considering it would have taken sandpaper and a fire hose to turn me into a woman again. Edging over to the newspapers, I listened

▲ *Even the garbage cans are bilingual in New Brunswick, Canada's only officially bilingual province.*

to the men talk while I scanned the Fredericton *Daily Gleaner.*

The rural New Brunswick accent is a mixture of Irish lilt, Yankee drawl and yowling tomcat. And it all comes out real slow. That's the English, anyway. The French always sound sophisticated, no matter what they're rattling on about. For example:

We say "bread," they say "*baguette.*"

We say "diner," they say "*café.*"

We say "twilight," which is a pretty good word. But they say "*entre chien et loup,*" which, roughly translated, means that narrow sliver of time between when the dogs stop barking and the wolves start howling.

Many New Brunswickers speak both French and English, often simultaneously. And it's not just the people, either. Every sign in the province — down to the instructions on roadside garbage cans — appears in both official languages.

Why? Because New Brunswick is 63 percent English and 33 percent French. No other province in Canada can boast such a healthy linguistic ratio — and healthy the relationship is between English and French in New Brunswick. But things weren't always so cosy here. Given their history, it's a wonder they're on speaking terms at all.

The Acadians

The French had been living in New Brunswick long before the Irish arrived. They arrived in the province, then part of a larger region called Acadia, in the 1600s.

The early Acadians were a simple, peaceful and industrious folk. Profoundly religious, these gentle people were communal by nature — they built dykes, cultivated their fields and fished as a group.

While the settlers were busy working the land, the British and French governments were fighting over who actually owned it. Control shifted back and forth, until the British finally won in 1713.

By this time, there were thousands of French people (by now called Acadians) living in the region. This was thousands too many, according to the British — which was why they started rounding the Acadians up, forcing them onto transport ships and deporting them in 1755.

Despite the best efforts of the British, many Acadians escaped deportation. Some made it as far as Quebec, while the rest hid out in the woods. By 1764, the Acadians were allowed to return home again. Broken in body and spirit, these homeless people travelled for months, often by foot, only to find English families living in their homes.

Fast-forward a few centuries, and approximately one-third of New Brunswick's population is now French-speaking. While it's impossible to right the injustices of the past, the province has implemented policies in recent years to ensure a more equitable future for all. One such initiative is the Official Languages of New Brunswick Act, passed in 1969.

This act decreed that most government services, both provincially and federally, must be offered in both official languages (by law, only federal services are bilingual in the rest of Canada). With one sweep of the pen, the law made New Brunswick Canada's only officially bilingual province — a historic and well-deserved milestone for the region's beleaguered Acadians.

When the men finally left the Irving station, I poured myself a *café*, loaded it up with *lait* and *sucre*, and headed back to the campground. That's when I met John Watling, my first fellow IAT hiker.

Learning from Trail Friends

I'd read about the lifelong friendships that people forge while hiking the Appalachian Trail. Hikers swap information about gear, alert each other to difficult areas ahead and offer a sympathetic ear when spirits flag. I'd looked forward to meeting people on the IAT, but the problem was there weren't any.

The IAT was still so new, few people knew about it. Even fewer have actually hiked it — less than ten since John Brinda became the first person to complete the trail in 1997. I knew of only seven other hikers who were hiking the IAT in 2000. Some were a few weeks ahead, while the rest were a few weeks behind. Knowing this, I wasn't expecting to meet a single hiker — which is why I was so delighted to meet John Watling.

When I met him, John had been walking for five months straight. His original plan had been to hike just the Appalachian Trail, which he had done. But rather than stopping at Mount Katahdin, the northern terminus of the Appalachian Trail, John had just kept on walking.

After months on the trail, John had hiking down to a science. He carried no extra gear, not even a pocket knife: "Too heavy." For eating, he carried a plastic spoon with a sawed-off handle: "Who needs a fork?" He didn't carry a shred of extra clothing, not even spare shoes: "If my boots get wet, they'll dry out eventually. Besides, they'll just get wet again anyway."

From meeting John, I realized that my obsession with the heaviness of my pack was normal. Experienced hikers are fanatical about weight because they've learned the hard way: hiking with a heavy pack is no fun.

Forget soul-searching and flower-gazing when you're staggering down the trail with a grand piano on your back. It's "Does God exist?" followed immediately by "I wonder what those aspirins weigh?" Or "Great view," then "Do I really NEED my tent?" Or "Wild onions," then "Hey — if I ate off the land, I wouldn't need a stove!"

Some hard-core hikers actually do travel without stoves. Doing so can restrict one's food choices, though. Rumour has it that one stoveless Appalachian Trail hiker ate nothing but dry breakfast cereal for five months, while another subsisted on potato chips and cake icing.

John was obsessive about weight, but he carried a stove — a tiny wire contraption that resembled a stick insect. On the Appalachian Trail, he'd used it to cook plain rice and noodles. "No salt. Didn't want the extra weight."

By the time I met him, John's obsession with weight had mellowed. From plain rice, he'd switched to blueberry pop tarts, instant noodles and caramel granola bars. In fact, the IAT had turned John into somewhat of a granola bar connoisseur.

"Stay away from the no-name brands," he said. "And avoid the banana bread flavour at all costs."

John had relaxed about weight, but only slightly. He explained that the less he carried, the lighter his pack was and the fewer calories he needed to consume. The fewer calories he consumed, the less food he needed and the lighter his pack would be.

"...And the lighter your pack, the faster you can walk and the happier you'll be," he concluded.

Despite shedding some gear at the start of my trip, my pack was still far too heavy. I decided to try and lighten my load. But after dumping my pack out, I saw that there wasn't much I could spare. So I cut the edges off my maps, squeezed out half my tube of toothpaste (that was John's inspired idea) and shortened the straps dangling from my backpack. Then I stuffed everything back in the pack and hoisted it onto my shoulders.

The pack was lighter, but not by much. That's when I realized that the problem wasn't the small things, it was the big things.

Shopping for a Rutabaga Tube Sock

Before tackling the IAT, I'd had very little hiking experience. I also had no hiking gear, which meant I had to face shopping in outdoor stores. For me, outdoor stores were like automobile repair shops — full of people who spout long-winded sentences that make little sense.

"Need a sleeping bag, eh? Well, there's yer double-quilted-fuel-injected-periwinkle variety, and then there's the reversible-rutabaga-tube-sock-with-baffle-construction. Which one'll it be?" Not only do you not understand a word, a quick glance at the price tag reveals that you can't afford it anyway.

If you explain that all you need is a good, reasonably priced sleeping bag, they look at you blankly. If you say that you're also looking for an inexpensive tent, stove and backpack, they usually stagger backwards, then run for the intercom.

"LUNATIC IN AISLE THREE!"

Wanting to avoid this embarrassment, I'd read hiking books, surfed the internet and pestered hiker friends for information. After several weeks, I'd compiled a detailed list. Then it was time to go shopping.

The first store didn't carry a single item on my list. Nor did the next, or the next. At that point, it was either hike in flip-flops and sleep in a garbage bag, or use my best judgement. As things turned out, I would have been better off hiking in flip-flops.

Every major purchase I'd made — backpack, tent, boots, sleeping bag and stove — was a mistake. All the items were solidly constructed and reasonably priced — but heavy. I didn't realize how heavy until I lifted John's backpack.

It flew onto my shoulders like a dove. That's because John's goose-down sleeping bag packed down to grapefruit size, while my synthetic sleeping bag resembled a watermelon. John slept on a skimpy three-quarter-length piece of foam, while I slept on an enormous, self-inflating mattress. John's pack was made of paper-thin nylon, while mine was built out of heavy Cordura, and so on.

When I complained about my heavy pack to John, he said, "The more you carry, the more you'll enjoy camping. The less you carry, the more you'll enjoy hiking."

I finished sorting through my pack, threw the extra gear into a box, then headed to the Plaster Rock post office to mail everything home.

Plaster Rock

Whoever named the town of Plaster Rock was certainly no poet. And with logging trucks hogging the roads and the Fraser Paper sawmill spewing noxious clouds into the sky, the town probably won't win many tourism awards, either — though they do try. Every year, there's an annual Fiddlehead Festival held here.

◄ *John "Best Man" Watling, the remarkable but ever-modest New Brunswicker who hiked both the Appalachian Trail and the IAT in 2000, a distance of over 4,000 kilometres.*

New Brunswickers are crazy about fiddleheads. A wild fern that resembles the scroll of a violin, they're found along riverbanks everywhere north of Virginia and east of the Mississippi.

Fiddleheads taste like a cross between asparagus and spinach. But to winter-weary New Brunswickers, they also taste like spring. Coaxed from the ground by the spring sun, fiddleheads seem to pop up overnight. Some say they appear so fast, you can actually hear them growing.

Teary Roadside Drama

After finishing my errands in town, I stopped by John's campsite for a brief visit, then turned in early.

By the time I got up the next morning, John had already left. We'd tentatively planned to meet in Riley Brook, almost forty kilometres away. I'd have to hurry to catch up with him. I packed my gear, had one last cup of coffee with the Irving boys, then headed down the road.

I passed a clapboard house with a line of flapping sheets outside, then a blue shack with a "BEWARE OF WIFE" sign nailed to the porch, then a tumbledown barn surrounded by dancing, wind-tossed daisies. After an hour, I'd walked over five kilometres. At that rate, I figured I'd beat John to Riley Brook.

Then my feet begin to burn. I'd forgotten how hard the road was underfoot. I stopped to drink some water from my canteen. It tasted like freshly squeezed tennis balls. Then I saw a boy on a bike across the road. Feeling tired and bored, I decided to go over and talk to him.

Halfway across the road, I heard angry knocking at the window of a nearby house. The boy's mother, face pinched with worry, was gesturing to the boy to come inside. The boy pedalled away with a terrified look on his face. I froze in the middle of the road. Did I really look that threatening?

I stood there, shoulders slumped, and looked down the highway. Heat waves flickered on the pavement ahead. I looked at the houses. The pretty little farmhouses suddenly looked like run-down hovels. I looked at my boots. I couldn't see my feet, but it felt like they were bleeding.

I walked to the side of the road, threw down my pack, sprawled out under a tree and started to cry.

I'd thought I would feel better once I'd lightened my pack, but I was wrong. The pack was still heavy, my feet were still sore, and I still had days of road walking ahead. Could I do it? Did I really want to?

That moment, sobbing by the side of the road, was my darkest hour on the IAT. I was finally starting to realize that hiking is as much a psychological journey as it is a physical one.

I had a good cry, then picked up my pack and started walking again.

A few hours later, I came to a little store. Inside, two people were sitting at the counter — a grizzled old man on one side, and the store clerk on the other. The silence between them was as tranquil as a quiet pond. I threw my pack down, grabbed a Coke from the fridge, plopped down beside the old man, ripped my boots off and start talking at top speed.

They stared at me, slack-jawed. I finished one Coke, and started another. After a few minutes, the old man stood up, stretched like a cat unfurling in front of a fireplace, then ambled out the door.

The door opened and closed, bringing a steady stream of locals to the stool beside me. Eventually, I pulled my boots back on and headed out into the heat again.

Trudging down the road in the searing heat, each step felt like its own 1,000-kilometre journey. Then a car slowed to a stop beside me.

"We saw you on the way into town. We figured we'd pick you up on the way back home. You wanna ride?" said an old man through the open window.

"That pack looks heavy. Jump in," urged the elderly woman beside him.

Yes! Yes! Yes! said my feet. "Thanks very much, but no," said my mouth.

"Want us to take your pack to Riley Brook, then?"

I thought long and hard about this, then regretfully declined. We talked for a few more minutes, then they started pulling away.

"Hey, wait!" I yelled.

Moments later, my pack and I were speeding down the highway. Leaning out the back window, I waggled my head in the wind like a happy hound dog. That's when I spotted John striding along the side of the road.

I hit the floor, praying the old man wouldn't stop. But of course he did.

"Hi, how are you — HEY! What are you doing in the car?" asked John.

▲ *Weathered barns and dancing wildflowers are a common sight in New Brunswick's Tobique Valley.*

Pleasant, modest and mild-mannered, John is one of those people who is impossible to dislike. But right then, I hated his guts. After walking for eight hours, John looked bright-eyed and fresh. By comparison, I'd hiked for six hours, had taken at least four breaks (one of which included a nervous breakdown) and was now crumpled in the car like a used Kleenex.

John refused the ride they offered (what a surprise), but accepted their invitation to camp in their yard.

▲ *An ingenious rolling bug repeller spotted near Riley Brook, New Brunswick*

Last of the Miller Clan

I was lying in my tent when John arrived an hour later. He pitched his tent, then we went in to say hello to Bob and Bernice Miller.

The Miller clan has lived in this area for generations. Today, there are only two families left: Bob and Bernice Miller, who ran the Riley Brook general store until retiring a few years ago, and Bill Miller, a well-known canoe-builder who lives with his mother a few kilometres away.

"Right near Bill's place is where the Miller Hotel used to be," Bob said, pointing to an old photograph hanging on the wall. "Babe Ruth stayed there. Mary Pickford too."

"That was back when the Tobique was a popular fishing destination," Bob continued. "The valley was thriving then — schools up and down the valley, and there was no shortage of work. But when they built the dam, the salmon declined and the tourists stopped coming. Now there's only old people here."

While Bob talked, Bernice moved around the kitchen, putting the kettle on to boil, setting cups on the table and pulling containers from the fridge. I snuck a peek at John. He appeared to be trying to listen to Bob while stalking Bernice and her Tupperware with hungry eyes.

Soon, we were washing slices of fresh bread down with mugs of sweet tea. I sat back, marvelling at how pleasant it was to be sitting in that kitchen, surrounded by new friends.

Miller Canoes

The next morning, John and I set out together. We made it to the Miller Canoe Shop, a few kilometres down the road. I decided to stop and investigate, while John opted to keep walking. So, after hugs goodbye and promises to write, we parted ways.

When I rang the bell at the Miller farmhouse, an old woman answered the door.

"I'm Wilma Miller," she said, not surprised to see me, as if grubby backpackers turned up at her door every day. "Hiking the IAT, are you? Interested in canoes? My son Bill's the canoe-builder. He'll be back soon. How about some water while you wait?"

I drained the glass while Mrs. Miller made tea and arranged some homemade cookies on a plate. When she set the cookies on the table, I resisted the temptation to grab the plate and tip the entire contents into my mouth.

Something odd had happened to my appetite. During the first few weeks of my hike, I'd been completely unable to eat. Now, I was hungry all the time. And no matter how much I ate, I kept losing weight. Bones I hadn't seen in years were popping out everywhere. These bones, combined with my scratched legs and perpetually sunburnt lips, gave me a sort of woodsy chic. Or so I thought.

Over tea, Mrs. Miller told me that Miller Canoes was one of the oldest wooden canoe companies in Canada. It all started back in 1925, when William Victor Miller built his first canoe in the attic of the Miller homestead. The business grew over the years, then William Victor Miller II took over in 1972. William Victor Miller III started helping his dad around the boat shop that same year, and is now the current owner of Miller Canoes.

There were two cookies left when we heard the clomp of heavy boots on the porch. The door swung open and a kind-faced man in his mid-fifties appeared.

"Hi Mum, whose backpack — hey! Hello! Hiking the IAT, are ya?" said William Victor Miller III, tossing his cap on the table.

Once the introductions were made, Bill sat down and reached for a cookie. Mrs. Miller poured him some tea, then asked about his trip to town.

"It was a real nice grave-digging, Mum," said Bill. "Everyone was there."

Bill explained that when someone dies in the Tobique region, everyone gathers to dig the grave.

"I like doing things that way," he said. "In fact, that's how the Miller boat shop was built. Eighty men turned up, and the building was up by sundown."

Bill offered to give me a tour of the shop. Casting a longing glance at the last remaining cookie, I followed him out of the house and across a field.

There was a sign nailed to a pole in the middle of the field: "Welcome to beautiful downtown Nictau." On the back, it said, "Thank you for visiting."

"This is it. Downtown Nictau," said Bill, flinging out his arms.

I looked around. The grassy field sparkled in the early morning sun. Crickets chirped. The air smelled of clover and freshly turned earth.

"Best thing about living in Nictau is I never get stuck in rush-hour traffic on my way to work," said Bill. "Well, except the other day, I had to wait for a deer to cross the field."

There was a grizzled golden retriever lolling in the doorway of the boat shop. "Meet Rusty," said Bill, stepping over the sleeping form, then disappearing inside. When my eyes adjusted to the gloom, I saw a sign: "If God had wanted fibreglass canoes, he would have made fibreglass trees."

Inside the shop, sawdust lay in drifts on the wide-planked floor, the workbench was littered with dead car batteries and paint cans, and wood was piled to the ceiling. But in the middle of the chaos, glowing like a summer sunset, was a partially built cedar-strip canoe.

Miller's shop might be messy, but every cedar strip on every Miller Canoe is lovingly placed — which is why he only builds eight or nine boats a year. But it wasn't always that way.

"Used to pump out almost fifty boats a year. Had to hire assistants and everything," said Bill. He found the experience stressful, plus the math didn't make sense. "Why make a boat in three days that's worth $150, when I can spend time making a nice one that sells for $3,000?"

In addition to taking his time, Bill uses nothing but home-grown wood for his canoes. Every fall, he climbs the hill behind the boat shop and cuts eastern white cedar for the ribs, white spruce for the gunwales and sturdy ash for the stem. Once the trees

Bill Miller, a third generation canoe-builder, holding a miniature Miller canoe at his boat shop in Nictau, New Brunswick ▶

are cut and limbed, Bill stacks the wood behind the boat shop, then lets it season for at least two years in the hot summer sun, the driving fall rains and the deep winter snows.

Bill takes a few months off after woodcutting, then returns — somewhat regretfully — to canoe-building again.

It's not that Bill dislikes canoe-building. Canoes are his life. But he also enjoys reciting Robert Service while poling down the Tobique River, browsing through the piles of books stacked around his armchair, and, above all, spinning a good yarn. The Murder on the Tobique story — complete with a flower-strewn corpse in a birch-bark canoe — is one of his favourites.

Murder on the Tobique

"It happened back in 1888," said Bill, absentmindedly unfurling a curl of cedar he'd picked off the dog.

The way Bill told it, Major and Mrs. Howes and their four children were on their annual fishing trip when the tragedy occurred. Susan Howes, a pretty and cultured woman in her thirties, was in the lead canoe when her boat rounded a sharp bend in the river. Two shots rang out in quick succession. Susan Howes didn't hear the next shot; she died the instant the third bullet entered her brain.

To this day, no one's quite sure who pulled the trigger, or what really happened, but this is the story.

On the night before the murder, Major Howes spotted two men spearing fish by torch light in his section of the river. He yelled at the men to go away, but they ignored him. So Howes jumped into a canoe with his son, who fired warning shots over the men's heads. The poachers fled downstream with Howes and son in hot pursuit. When the men disappeared from sight, the Howeses gave up and went home.

The poachers were Frank Trafton and Henry Phillipin. The next day, Frank and Henry decided to teach Howes a lesson. If Howes could scare them, well they could scare Howes right back. They took their guns to Robertson's Bend, cut a hole in the underbrush, and waited for Howes to appear.

We know what happened next. But why were the men out fishing in the middle of the night? Because Henry Phillipin's brothers and sisters were starving. They'd been living on catfish and potatoes. Enduring such poverty would be hard on anyone, but it was especially difficult for the Phillipins.

The Phillipins had once lived a life of ease and luxury. Phillipin Senior had been a prosperous London banker until his firm failed in 1880. He decided to immigrate to Canada and make a fresh start. "Let's take the children to Halifax," he said to his wife. Apparently she didn't think much of the idea, and promptly deserted him.

Undeterred, Phillipin Senior went to Halifax with his children in tow. He found a job, but the company failed soon after. He tried farming in Nova Scotia, but that didn't go well either. Finally, he bought some land along the Tobique River, left his children there to farm it, and returned to Halifax to try cider manufacturing.

Then the poor man dropped dead, leaving five penniless orphans stranded on the Tobique River.

Sitting there in the bushes at Robertson Bend, Henry Phillipin was smarting with righteous indignation at being driven off by the Howeses. But was he mad enough to kill?

The canoe rounded the bend. The men fired their guns. The Howeses fired back. A gunfight ensued. When the smoke cleared, Susan Howes was dead. This much we do know. We also know that the locals — who felt terrible about the whole thing — strewed wildflowers into the birch-bark canoe containing Susan Howes' remains. And we also know that, although Phillipin and Trafton swore they shot too high to kill anyone, they were charged with manslaughter and sent to jail.

But who actually killed her? In Bill's version of the story, Major Howes sat bolt upright on his deathbed, confessed to shooting his wife for the inheritance money, and then died. Whatever the true story is, some feel the tragedy was inevitable.

After the murder, a local remarked to a newspaper reporter, "The Tobique settlers feel that the fish in the stream which flows past their doors should be as free as the air they breathe ... They don't like to see strangers coming in and taking what they think is theirs ... Very little was needed to fan the smouldering spark into a flame."

Today, the story is all but forgotten in the Tobique region. Bill knows it because up in the eaves of his barn is a very special birch-bark canoe. It isn't the one that carried Susan Howes to her grave, but it was built by Frank Lockwood, one of the Indian guides leading the Howeses' fishing expedition that day.

We climbed to the top of the barn — the heat intensified with every rung of the ladder — and Bill threw off a burlap sheet covering an old birch-bark canoe.

Birch-bark canoes

Said to be one of the most perfect Aboriginal inventions, birch-bark canoes were made by building a frame of wooden ribs, then covering it with sheets of birch bark, white side facing in. Everything was lashed together using split tree roots, and hot pine pitch was used to seal the seams. Moved along by paddle or pole, these lightweight craft could speed along in just a few inches of water. For less water than that, the boats were fitted with "canoe shoes" and dragged over the rocks. In theory, anyway. Watching Bill replace the burlap with a fatherly pride, I couldn't imagine staying afloat in such a frail-looking craft.

I hung out at Bill's place for a few days, "helping out" in the boat shop, paddling on the Tobique, and eating several of Mrs. Miller's fine home-cooked meals. Then, finally, it was time to go. Setting off for Mount Carleton Park, I left doubly blessed: it was a gorgeous summer day and I'd made two wonderful new friends.

Boundless Wilderness

At 820 metres, Mount Carleton is the highest point in the Maritimes. Softened by glaciers, this once jagged peak dominates New Brunswick's Appalachian mountain range.

They say you can see ten million trees from the summit. I don't know about that, because the day I climbed Carleton, I counted more raindrops than trees. Still, cloaked in mist, the surrounding peaks — Head (792 metres), Sagamook (777 metres) and Bailey (564 metres) — looked ancient and mysterious.

More impressive than the mountains, though, was the sight of endless wilderness stretching off in all directions. Except for a single road winding through the trees, there was no sign of civilization: no houses, no TV antennas, no telephone poles, no anything.

I tried to imagine being a settler, crashing around in that lonely forest, trying to carve out a new life. But the land was too big, too empty, too ... too ...

There is no word that adequately describes the insignificance one feels when confronted by endless wilderness. We're talking wilderness here, not park land. Parks — no matter how large or wild — have nice, neat borders around them. They have signs and rules, forest rangers and entrance fees. Parks have an address.

◄ *Fog lingering over Nepisiguit Lakes and surrounding hills in Mount Carleton Provincial Park*

They are somewhere.

The wilderness is nowhere. Next to nowhere, there's just more nowhere. And your presence in that nowhere amounts to exactly nothing. Surrounded by wilderness — as you are on Mount Carleton — you realize you're just one of billions of organisms scattered on the earth's surface. It's a realization that's both humbling and exhilarating.

The Unlucky Loyalists

The New Brunswick wilderness may have terrified the Loyalists who settled here, but not as much as the terror they fled.

When the American War of Independence ended in 1783, thousands of Americans who'd remained loyal to the British Crown suddenly found themselves on the losing side. Fearing vengeance from the victorious rebels, the Loyalists scooped up their belongings — including essentials such as damask tablecloths and heirloom silver — and ran. About 14,000 made it as far as present-day New Brunswick. Many settled at the mouth of the Saint John River, while others moved up the river and its tributaries.

Life was rough for the Loyalist refugees. Used to milder weather and finer living, they shivered through their first winter in tents and clumsily built cabins. Some died of smallpox. But with help from the Native people, they gradually adapted to life in the wilderness.

In 1883, a man named Edward Jack dreamed of creating a park to commemorate the 100th anniversary of the Loyalist landing in New Brunswick. It took almost a hundred years, but Mount Carleton finally became a provincial park in 1970.

After eating lunch on Mount Carleton, I followed the faded trail markings across the summit, then headed over the side of the mountain. Soon, I was walking through alpine blueberries and Labrador tea.

Labrador tea — also called Hudson's Bay spice — is a small, aromatic shrub with shiny, oblong leaves. The leaves are high in vitamin C, which the native peoples once used for medicinal tea. I picked a handful to try that night, then tested a few blueberries. Still unripe, they were hard and tasted bitter.

"So much for living off the land," I thought, heading down the hill.

I camped beside Nictau Lake that night. Mount Carleton loomed on the opposite shore, a brooding hulk in the gathering dusk. I sat by the lake and watched the smoke from my campfire drift across the lake. Then the stars came out, one after the other. I tiptoed to bed around midnight, reluctant to break the stillness with the crash of my footsteps.

The next day, I had two options: walk or hitchhike to St. Quentin, where I planned to buy food for the Restigouche section. Walking would mean three days of dodging logging trucks on a deserted country road. Hitchhiking would mean arriving in one hour.

I stuck out my thumb. An hour later, I was shopping for supplies in St. Quentin. Hitchhiking was so pleasant, I decided to stop road walking for the rest of the IAT.

After re-supplying in St. Quentin, I headed back to the highway and stuck out my thumb. Three hours later, I was canoeing down the Restigouche River.

The Restigouche River

There are two ways through the Restigouche section of the trail. The official IAT route involves a tough five-day hike along a poorly marked trail ("The worst trail I saw in 2,000 miles," John said when I saw him later). An alternate route involves throwing your pack into a canoe and gliding down a wild river for three days.

Hmmm. Tough choice.

The best thing about the Restigouche — beside the fact that 55 kilometres of this 200-kilometre river is part of the Canadian Heritage River System — is that you might find yourself paddling next to prime ministers, New York bankers, famous entertainers or even a U.S. president.

The Restigouche River is one of the most exclusive fishing hideaways in North America. It's what the Tobique might have become, had the river not been dammed a half century ago. The banks are dotted with sprawling log mansions. Many were designed by Stanford White, the renowned New York architect who designed Madison Square Gardens.

Ironically, Stanford White was shot to death in 1906 by a jealous husband in that very building. White had been having an affair with the man's wife, actress

▲ *Heavily-loaded hikers struggle up a steep hill in the IAT's dreaded Restigouche section.*

Evelyn Nesbitt. White's affair with Nesbitt — which was exceedingly sordid from all accounts — was later chronicled in the 1950s film *The Girl in the Red Velvet Swing.*

Money, power and sex scandals — it's all there on the Restigouche. That and the more serious business of fishing. But for today's fishermen, a trip to the Restigouche is no backwoods affair.

The fishermen, known locally as "sports," do their fishing from handcrafted cedar-strip canoes. Every morning, uniformed fishing guides whisk the sports to private fishing holes. After a few hours of fishing, the sports are returned to the lodge and served an elegant lunch. Afternoons are spent reading, chatting and snoozing in luxurious lounges, then it's back to fishing at dusk, followed by another fine meal.

William's Falls in New Brunswick's Mount Carleton Provincial Park ▶

A handful of absurdly rich people own much of the land along the Restigouche. There are places where locals can fish, but they are few and far between. Some resent this, but many more welcome the well-heeled visitors.

"We're as glad to see the sports come to fish in the month of June as when Santa Claus comes down the stove pipe on the 25th day of December," one local commented.

That's because the sports drop millions of dollars into New Brunswick's economy during the annual fishing season. But the locals don't just appreciate them for their money. Over the years, the sports have fought to protect their wilderness playground. As a result, Restigouche is completely unspoiled today. The river is full of prized Atlantic salmon, while coyotes, black bears, deer and moose roam through the woods. Even provincially endangered species, such as lynx and osprey, have been spotted here.

I didn't see much wildlife on the Restigouche, though. I was too busy ogling the millionaires. I passed a canoe anchored at Million Dollar Pool. Said to be the best fishing hole on the river, it's owned by the Restigouche Salmon Club, the oldest fishing club in North America. Two men stood motionless in the canoe. They were staring at the water so hard they didn't see me. The guide did, though. Waving his arms and scowling, he gestured at my paddle as I floated by.

I figured he meant I was scaring off the fish, which was fine, because I didn't feel much like paddling anyway. Putting the offending article away, I lay back and propped my feet on my backpack. "Now this is more like it," I thought, watching trees whizzing by on the riverbanks.

Late afternoon, I passed five men on a sandbar. They were drinking beer, splashing each other and pretending to push each other into the river. They froze when they saw me — beer cans half-raised to mouths, wet jeans plastered to legs, mouths frozen into "O's."

I waved, but no one moved. I looked over my shoulder a few minutes later, but they were still frozen like a tableau of salt pillars. Just call me Sodom.

I camped at one of the river's designated campsites that night. The five men arrived an hour later. They landed on the beach, then bounded up the riverbank and surrounded my picnic table. No one said a word until I put my book down and smiled. Then the floodgates opened.

Who was I? Why was I travelling alone as a woman? Wasn't I scared? Wasn't I afraid of bears? "Wouldn't catch me out here alone," said one guy with a shiver. "By the way, what are you having for supper?" When I told him, he shivered again, then invited me to join them.

Soon I was tucking into a steak, mashed potatoes and fresh green beans. Someone handed me a beer, then another. Dessert was thick slices of molasses cake baked by one of the men's wives.

"She always makes us a cake when we go on our annual fishing trip," he explained.

Friends since childhood, the men get together every year to paddle down the Restigouche. Maybe it was the beer, maybe it was the smoke from the nearby campfire, but the men's eyes grew misty when they talked about the Restigouche.

"She's a beautiful, beautiful river," they said. And it was. Bands of purple and gold soared across the clear night sky, while below, the water laughed and whispered over the rocks.

Calmness drifted into my rumpled soul that night. It didn't last until morning, but it returns whenever I think of the Restigouche.

The men were still sleeping when I pushed off the next morning. They'd been up all night, giggling and singing drunkenly beneath the pines. After another day of gliding down the river, I crossed the Quebec border. I left my canoe in Matapédia, then began the last — and most remarkable — part of my journey.

Sunset over New Brunswick's famed Restigouche River ▶

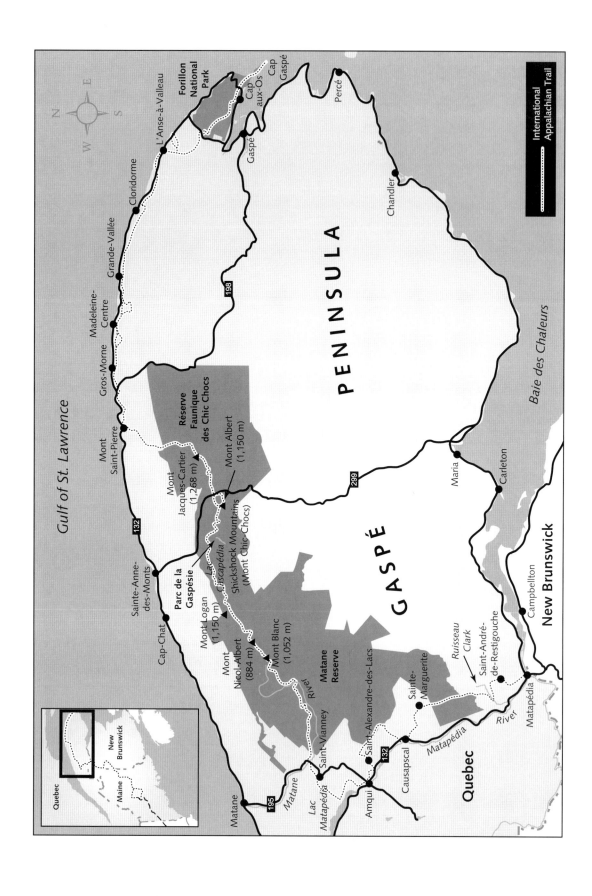

Gulf of St. Lawrence

N
W   E
S

Forillon National Park

L'Anse-à-Valleau

Cap aux-Os

Cloridorme

Cap Gaspé

Grande-Vallée

Gaspé

Madeleine-Centre

Gros-Morne

Percé

Mont Saint-Pierre

198

Chandler

Réserve Faunique des Chic Chocs

Mont Jacques-Cartier (1,268 m)

PENINSULA

Mont Albert (1,150 m)

Sainte-Anne-des-Monts

132

Shickshock Mountains (Mont Chic-Chocs)

Lac Cascapédia

299

Parc de la Gaspésie

Maria

Cap-Chat

Mont Logan (1,150 m)

Mont Nicol-Albert (884 m)

Mont Blanc (1,052 m)

Carleton

Matane Reserve

GASPÉ

River

Ruisseau Clark

Matane

Saint-Vianney

Saint-Alexandre-des-Lacs

Sainte-Marguerite

Saint-André-de-Restigouche

Campbellton

195

Matane

Lac Matapédia

Amqui

132

Causapscal

Matapédia River

Matapédia

New Brunswick

Quebec

Baie des Chaleurs

Quebec

Maine

New Brunswick

International Appalachian Trail

QUEBEC

Love, Loathing and Fear

So far on the IAT, I had experienced love, loathing and fear: love for all the wonderful people I'd met, loathing for all the road walking I'd done, and a vast, irrational fear of mad rapists. While the love and loathing were real, the rapists were not. I'd created them, which wasn't surprising given that hiking provides endless hours of reflection.

Then I arrived in Quebec. Suddenly I had something real to worry about. After New Brunswick, the IAT abruptly veers off the road and descends into one of the wildest stretches of wilderness in North America. Ahead, I would encounter rugged mountains, windswept tundra and plenty of old-growth forest. There would be the usual array of wild critters, with one important addition: Canada's southernmost caribou herd lives in Quebec. These animals live atop the Shickshock Mountains, a remote and secret world of alpine wildflowers, blue and scarlet berries, and ancient, pockmarked boulders.

Caribou, rugged mountains and old-growth forests: this, then, was real hiking. The problem was, I wasn't a real hiker. I'd done all right so far, because let's face it

The village of Matapédia, Quebec, surrounded by brilliant autumn foliage ▶

— it's pretty hard to get lost on a road. But real hiking? With a map and one of those compass thingies?

The trouble was, my compass skills ranged from rusty to non-existent, I didn't have key maps for the Quebec section, and worst of all, the IAT was still a work in progress. In some places, I wasn't sure there was a trail at all.

There was one section in Quebec that had me particularly worried: the Matane Reserve. Before leaving for my trip, I called several people on the IAT phone list to ask (a) whether the trail was finished through the Matane Reserve (b) if it was finished, whether it was sufficiently blazed, and (c) how long it would take to hike, if and when it was finished.

"Don't even think about going through the Matane," one person said. "The trail's not finished yet. It's too dangerous. You'll get lost for sure."

"It'll take you six days to hike it," another said. "It's a nice, easy walk."

"Four days," said a third. "And wear an orange hunting vest if you go during hunting season, so you don't get shot by mistake."

The information I found on the internet was even less reassuring. According to Marvin Higgins, who'd hiked the IAT in 1999:

> "The trail was sporadically marked ... We took wrong turns several times
> ... Signs had been vandalised. Three or four signposts had no signs at all ...
> In several places, the trail was closed with ferns and bushes and tall grasses
> as a result of not being tread on by human feet. It seemed a highway for
> moose, not humans."

If Higgins' account was grim, the things he'd seen used to mark the trail were worse. In addition to the official blue-and-white aluminum blazes (which include the letters "IAT" for International Appalachian Trail and "SIA" for Sentier international des Appalaches, the French equivalent), Higgins had followed:

- blue paint on trees
- white paint on trees
- blue-and-white paint on trees
- orange flagging tape
- pink flagging tape

- blue flagging tape
- cairns
- stumps
- string

"String. Right. Wonder what colour," I thought, shutting off the computer. Then I'd gone in search of my boyfriend.

"The trail is rugged, untouched and pristine," I began. "You'd love it. Especially the Matane section." I paused for a moment, then added, "If you don't come with me, I'll probably fall in a crevasse and die."

My boyfriend agreed to hike with me through the Matane Reserve. In fact, he was really excited about the idea. He'd take a vacation from work and meet me at the beginning of the reserve. Much relieved, I didn't give it another thought until I arrived in Matapédia, the first village in Quebec on the IAT.

Matapédia

Matapédia means "where the rivers meet" in the local Indian dialect, a fitting description for a town built at the junction of the Restigouche and Matapédia rivers. After pulling the canoe up on the beach, I went in search of David LeBlanc, who apparently had some maps for me.

Finding hiking maps for the IAT had been difficult. The Maine section of the IAT didn't have any, so I'd followed a road map. The New Brunswick section had sent me photocopied topographic maps. They weren't real hiking maps, but someone had drawn in the IAT with red pencil.

Quebec was the only section with proper hiking maps. The trouble was, they didn't cover the Matane Reserve, they were only available in French, and they didn't have any when I called. The person on the phone explained that more maps were being printed. When the new ones were ready, they would send me a set to David LeBlanc's place in Matapédia.

"Who's David LeBlanc?" I asked. "How do you know he'll be there when I get there?" After all, I was talking to someone at IAT Quebec's head office in Matane. How did they know what some guy would be doing in Matapédia, several hundred kilometres away, several weeks in the future?

▲ *Herd of woodland caribou in the Parc de la Gaspésie*

"Oh, he'll be there," the person had said.

I found the informality of this arrangement a little disconcerting. I would have preferred to get the maps at an information booth, from someone wearing a shiny name tag and a freshly pressed uniform.

I didn't find David LeBlanc in Matapédia — he found me. The village is so small, it's easy to spot strangers — especially when they're standing in the bank wearing a backpack.

"Hey! Hiking the IAT?" I heard. Turning around, I saw a tall, serious-looking man in his mid-twenties.

I liked David immediately. Owner of an outdoor adventure company, David was also an enthusiastic supporter of the IAT. Much to my relief, he'd received my maps. But when we went to pick them up, I saw they were badly printed and difficult to read. A dart of fear shot through my heart.

"Here, I've got a map for you," said David, pulling out a hand-drawn map. Then, talking at top speed, he underlined problem areas, circled things, drew arrows and scribbled vital information in the margins. The map was a testament to David's enthusiasm for the IAT, but I wasn't sure I could follow it.

I thanked David for everything, then checked into the Matapédia Youth Hostel.

Rush hour, downtown Causapscal, Quebec, on the Matapédia River ▲

Run by a silver-haired man with sad eyes, the place was clean, cheap and pleasant. The old fellow dropped jugs of ice water at my door, brought me extra pillows, and politely refrained from mentioning the muddy swamp I'd created in his bathroom.

After my shower, I slept for almost two days straight. By the afternoon of the third day, I felt well rested and ready to leave. I shopped for supplies, fixed some gear, then dropped by David's place to say goodbye. While I was there, he invited me for supper.

"My girlfriend has the night off work, and some friends are dropping by," he said. "We'll cook you up some Gaspé specialties before you leave: pan-fried shrimps, maple sugar pie, the works."

Dinner sounded great, but it was several hours away. To fill time, I took a walk around the village.

They say that in Quebec, if you throw a stone in any direction, you'll break a church window. This isn't quite true of Matapédia. There's only one church here, but it towers above the village like a watchful parent — a constant reminder of how important the Catholic Church once was in this province.

In the early 1900s, French-Canadians were deeply religious, poorly educated and largely rural. Many were labourers for English-owned businesses. Then, in mid-century, things began to change. French-Canadian intellectuals began criticising English domination, and speaking out against the smothering influence of the Catholic Church. Finally in 1960, Jean Lesage was voted in as Quebec's new premier, and the Quiet Revolution began.

The sixties were a time of radical social change in North America, but especially in Quebec. In a few short years, Lesage's government pulled the province out of the dark ages (*la grande noirceur*) by wresting control of health, education and welfare from the Church and creating state-owned industries to reduce the financial domination of the English. These were heady times in the province, a time when anything was possible — even the idea of a separate Quebec nation.

René Lévesque, who was part of Lesage's government, believed that Quebec independence was essential to end the cultural and economic domination of the English. After leaving Lesage's government, Lévesque formed the Parti Québécois, the separatist party that ultimately held Quebec's first referendum on sovereignty in 1980.

To Lévesque's dismay, voters rejected separation by a wide margin. When Lévesque died some years later, his dream of a Quebec nation remained very much alive. Another referendum was held in 1995. The Quebec nationalists lost once again, but this time the vote was a knuckle-biting 49.4 to 50.6. Just a few more "yes" votes, and Quebec would have become a separate country.

Like most English-speaking Quebeckers, I voted "no" in the 1995 referendum. Without wading through four centuries of history, my view is that Canada would be far a duller place without the lively and passionate French-Canadians.

Today, the mere mention of the word "separation" brings a glassy look to people's eyes. Few Quebeckers want to relive that dreadful day when Quebec almost became a country, or Canada was almost destroyed, depending on how they voted. I certainly didn't want to talk separation with David LeBlanc, but then there it was, a bucket of ice water splashed over a fine dinner.

"So, are you a federalist?" David asked. "That's too bad. The separatist movement's so strong, we'll have our own country soon."

My hackles rose and my opinion of him plummeted — not for being a separatist, but for bringing up a taboo subject. There's an unwritten rule in Quebec: federalists and separatists never discuss politics. The conversation, mostly in English, limped around the issue for awhile. I tried using my limited French, but that was a disaster, because the conversation just galloped away without me. By the end of the evening, I was in a foul mood.

"Bloody Quebec politics," I thought, storming back to the hostel after supper. I was still muttering angrily when a man on a bicycle appeared. He stared at me as he rode past, then stopped a few metres ahead.

"Hiking the IAT?" he asked when I was within earshot.

I don't know how he knew, but I was in no mood to find out.

"*Oui*," I replied, without slowing down.

The man looked worried. "I wouldn't go on that trail, and I'm from around here," he said. "The trail's not well marked. Pretty confusing in spots."

That got my attention. I showed the guy the map that David had drawn for me.

"David knows this country like the back of his hand," he said, squinting at the map, "but I don't know about this map ..."

The man pulled a map out of his pocket. It was similar to the one that David had given me, but this one was covered with squiggly red, yellow and blue pencil lines.

"Take this," he said. "It's my own map. Maybe it'll help if you get lost."

Lost in the Raspberries

I left Matapédia with fourteen maps. I got lost within the first hour.

One minute I was wandering through a dappled maple forest, and the next I was thrashing through shoulder-high raspberry bushes. Deeper and deeper I went, searching for the trail. Then I stopped, scratched and bleeding, at the top of a small hill.

Off to the left, I saw a line of trees with orange plastic ribbons (called flagging tape) tied to the branches. The waves of panic started to recede, then I spotted a line of trees marked with pink flagging tape off to the right. Then I saw some blue flagging tape off in the distance.

I pulled out David's map, but it was no help because I hadn't been following it. I pulled out a compass, but that was useless because I didn't know where I was on the map. Then I pulled out a roll of red flagging tape: this I knew how to use.

Retracing my steps back through the raspberry bushes, I tied pieces of red ribbon every few feet. Progress was slow, but the line of fluttering markers was a reassuring sight. Twenty minutes later, I was standing on the trail again. Much relieved, I vowed to keep track of my location on the map at all times.

The Mountains with the Restless Heart

The Matapédia Valley is the western edge of Quebec's Gaspé Peninsula. Called *Gaspeg* or "land's end" by the Mi'kmaq Indians, the peninsula is a narrow limestone finger poking into the Atlantic Ocean.

▲ *An aerial view of Cap Gaspé*

Once described as a "vast sea of frozen mountains," the Gaspé is 21,000 square kilometres of rugged, inaccessible highlands. These highlands are an extension of the northern Appalachians, a chain of mountains that stretches from Alabama to Newfoundland. The Appalachians are among the oldest mountains on earth. But while they look solid and eternal, they're actually faking it. Chip through the rock to the mountain's core, and you'll find a restless heart.

Hundreds of million of years ago, the North American and European continents crashed into each other. On impact, a ridge of rock was pushed up. These were the first Appalachian Mountains.

The continents slowly drifted apart, then, several million years later, began moving back together again. On the return journey, sediment on the ocean floor was scraped up and heaped on North America, forming another line of mountains. The continents floated apart, then collided yet again, and another row of mountains was created.

During each of these orogenies (a geological term for mountain ranges formed by the intense upheavals of the earth's crust), the older mountains were shoved inland — which, in my opinion, is very un-mountainlike behaviour. If there's one thing that shouldn't gallop around, it's mountains. But move they did, which is why there are several parallel ridges, valleys and plateaus in the Appalachian chain.

Saint-André-de-Restigouche

The trail left the maple forest, cut through some farmers' fields, then came out beside the church in the village of Saint-André-de-Restigouche. Setting my pack down, I sat down on the church steps for awhile.

After two days in the darkened woods, it was great being out in the open again. Farmers' fields rolled off in all directions, and to the north, a line of mountains rose on the horizon. As I sat there gazing at the far-off hills, an old guy drove by in a clattery old car. He stopped when he saw me, then backed up on the deserted main street. He got out of the car and strolled towards me, leaving

▲ *One of the IAT's many new overnight shelters*

the car door swinging on its hinges in the middle of the road.

It took several minutes to figure out what the old man was saying, but I eventually determined that he'd met two IAT hikers last year, and that he'd given them a ride to where the trail heads into the woods again, a few kilometres away. Then the old fellow offered me a ride, saying he was headed that way to pick blueberries.

I felt very clever figuring all this out, and lucky as well. Getting a ride meant skipping another section of road walking.

The blueberry picker dropped me off at the start of the trail. The path ran along an overgrown power line, then followed a confusing network of old roads — all of which were described, down to the metre — on the map that David had drawn for me.

The trail led me farther and farther from civilization. A light rain began to fall, casting a desolate pall over the landscape. Then the trail headed down to a river, where I found an IAT campsite. It was almost dark, so I decided to camp there for the night. Built into a protective circle of trees, the campsite consisted of several tent platforms, an outhouse and a fire pit. This was one of several new campsites built by IAT Quebec.

So far, the Canadian government has invested $3 million in the IAT project in Quebec. At first glance, the money seems out of proportion to the handful of hikers who've hiked the trail so far. But according to some marketing projections, the IAT could soon attract up to 100,000 hikers every year, generating many new jobs and millions of dollars of economic spin-offs — welcome news for a region where unemployment hovers around 20 percent.

Spooky Section

I was on the trail by 6:00 a.m. the next morning, far earlier than usual. But there was something spooky about where I was camped. Maybe it was the mist, thick as porridge, or maybe it was just being out there alone. Whatever the reason, I was down the trail, across the river and up the mountain on the other side in record time.

By the time I got to the top of the mountain, rays of sun were poking through the mist. The trail snaked back down the mountain, then stopped in front of a wide, rushing stream.

The Assemetquagan River wasn't very deep, but the bottom was covered in smooth, slippery boulders. Leaving my shoes on for traction, I started wading through the torrent with doll-like steps. If I slipped and broke a leg, it might be days before someone found me.

I crossed the river without mishap, but when I got to the other side I couldn't find the trail. The water made a hollow rushing sound around my legs as I stood there, staring at the bushes. The brush was so thick, there was nowhere to climb up on the bank. I sloshed up and down, then finally, desperate to escape the freezing water, I grabbed a bush and pulled myself up, falling forward into the bushes. I lay there with my pack on and my legs poking out, waiting for my legs to thaw out.

Within seconds, my legs were bright red and horrible itchy, causing me to leap back in the water and continue my search. I found the trail eventually, though I almost missed it. There were no trail markers and the opening through the bushes was barely visible. I festooned the trees with red flagging tape for the hikers behind me, then started walking again.

Trail Magic

It was almost dark when the trail came to a logging road. I walked through the rough, torn-up country, searching for a place to camp. Then a pick-up truck drove by, slowed down and stopped.

Anyone who doesn't believe in trail magic obviously hasn't been rescued by a gallant logger on a deserted road at sunset.

Trail magic is leaving your pocket knife at a campsite, then having someone return it to you 300 kilometres down the trail; or running dangerously low on food on the trail, then meeting a hiker carrying dozens of Snickers bars. These things happened to me, but most long-distance hikers tell similar tales of divine luck.

Trail magic is more than a lesson about appreciating the kindness of strangers. It's really about finding yourself in a situation of need, then allowing — though never expecting — perfect strangers to rescue you.

The logger who stopped was headed home at the end of his shift. He drove me to Causapscal, 20 kilometres away, then dropped me off at the municipal campground. After waving goodbye, I walked to the phone booth and called my boyfriend. The

An aerial view of the northern Appalachians ▶

last few days had been challenging, and I needed to hear a comforting voice. I also wanted to discuss our hike through the Matane section, as it was less than a week away.

His voice was cracked and tired when he answered the phone. We talked for a few minutes, then he dropped the bomb:

"Monique, I can't go with you through the Matane Reserve," he said. "I can't even walk to the kitchen. I've got pneumonia."

What To Do?

After hanging up, I lingered in the phone booth, reluctant to leave the shining cubicle and enter the darkness. A fly crawled up the glass. I killed it. The neon light buzzed and flickered. I banged it with my fist, trying to make the noise stop. Then I started to cry.

My boyfriend was too sick to hike the Matane Reserve. Should I go by myself, or just give up? But going alone seemed crazy: I had no maps, I had no idea how long it would take. Heck, I didn't even know if the trail was finished.

After a sleepless night, I got out of the tent, yawning, scratching and rubbing my face. Then I scratched my face again, then again. Why was my face so itchy? And my left eye! Why was it so puffy and hot? After a frantic search for a mirror, I saw a mass of oozing red welts covering my left cheek.

Great. Poison ivy. On top of everything else.

I went into town to buy some lotion, but had no idea what "poison ivy" was in French. At the drugstore, my vigorous pantomime gathered a crowd, but failed to produce the necessary salve. I went back outside, sat on a bench and scratched. Eventually, I decided to take the bus to Amqui, 15 kilometres away. Once there, I would buy some salve and make a final decision about the Matane Reserve.

When I got to Amqui, I checked into a hotel and headed downtown. Once my errands were done, I started making phone calls.

First I called my boyfriend to see how he was doing. He didn't answer the phone, so I assumed he was sleeping. Next, I tried to find someone else to come with me through the Matane Reserve. An hour later, I'd run through my list of friends. I tried calling my boyfriend again, but he still wasn't home. I was starting to worry.

I wandered around the town for several hours, endlessly deliberating my options.

Eventually I ended up back at the hotel, where I plunked myself in front of the TV. Midway through the night, I tried calling my boyfriend again. This time he answered, but his voice was so wheezy and thin I could barely hear him. He'd been at the hospital all day. The doctor had prescribed plenty of bed rest, saying it could be months before he was well again. Then he cut the conversation short, saying he was too tired to talk.

By the end of the night, I'd made my decision. I was going home. I fell asleep with the TV blaring.

Do or Die

I'm not sure what happened in the night, but the next morning, I put my boots on, picked up my pack and headed out to buy hiking supplies.

Besides cooking chicken soup and hovering at his bedside, there was nothing I could do to hasten my boyfriend's recovery. Book or no book, I didn't want a half-completed hike haunting me for the rest of my life. I would hike through the Matane Reserve alone.

I didn't have a map for the Matane section, so I stopped at a gas station and bought a road map. It was 125 kilometres across the Matane Reserve, then another fifty kilometres through the Parc de la Gaspésie to where there was a road cutting north/south through the park.

Route 299 is one of the few roads through the Shickshock Mountains. With their troughs and folds of rock and lack of natural passes, these mountains were a formidable barrier — not just for me, but for early explorers as well. They were so rugged, it wasn't until 1844 that Sir William Logan became one of the first non-natives to explore the region. A few settlers moved in when the road was built, but this mountainous region remains largely uninhabited — which is why the Gîte du Mont Albert is such an oddity.

Located in the Parc de la Gaspésie, the Gîte is a luxurious inn, complete with brilliant French chef, right in the middle of the Shickshocks. As I struggled across howling tundra, inched past yawning chasms and slithered down treacherous water-falls over the next eight days, the inn grew into a paradise of mythic proportions. I also planned the meal I'd have, down to the toothpicks, when (and if) I survived.

▲ *Rolling hills and waist-high foliage in Quebec's Matane Reserve*

Getting ready to leave Amqui, though, the Gîte seemed as tiny and distant as a far-off star. I bought food and supplies, called home one last time, then phoned for a taxi. An hour later, I was standing in front of the check-in booth at the Matane Reserve. It was pouring rain.

The Matane Reserve

I don't know why there's a check-in booth at the reserve, because the woman just shook her head and looked suspicious when I asked to sign the hiking register. There was no hiking register. Knowing my name might make them responsible for me, and given that the place was plastered with pictures of hungry-looking bears, that wasn't something they were interested in.

Adding to my growing sense of foreboding, the woman didn't utter a single word the entire time I was in there, though she reluctantly slid a map of the reserve across the counter when I asked. It was an excellent map with the IAT clearly indicated, but between the mute woman, the gigantic bears, and the pouring rain, the Matane just didn't look promising. A few minutes later, I was standing at the trailhead.

I looked at my watch. It was four o'clock. My plan had been to camp at the trailhead and get an early start. But what was I going to do in my tent? Crawl inside and panic? I lifted the pack and headed up the hill.

Snug overnight cabin atop Mont Blanc in Quebec's Matane Reserve ▲

The trail went straight up for a few kilometres, then levelled off. Stopping to catch my breath, I spotted the shimmer of Lac Matane far, far below. After a quick break, I followed the steep trail for another few kilometres, then descended to a small lake.

It was nearly dark by the time I got there and the rain had turned into a full-blown storm. Luckily, there was a campsite nearby, including two half-built tent platforms and an enormous outhouse.

Rain lashed my face as I struggled with the tent. Once it was up, I made a dash for the outhouse with my gear. The building was dry and clean, and best of all, it had never been used. I cooked a pot of noodles on the floor, then ate supper sitting on the throne, feeling ever so smug as I listened to the rain hammering on the roof. Then I dashed to my tent, peeled off my wet clothes and fell asleep to the sound of a wind-tossed branch pecking against the tent.

The next day, the trail went straight up for hours. Stopping often to catch my breath, I picked blueberries, lay under trees, and lingered far longer than necessary over especially fine views. Then, midway between Mont Pointu and Mont Craggy, I met four hikers. I was so happy to see them, I practically licked their faces. I was sure I'd be alone out there, and here I was meeting people my second day out. Better still, they had walked the reserve several times, and one had actually worked on the trail as a volunteer.

They laughed when I told them about how worried I'd been. According to them, the trail was well-marked, straightforward and absolutely superb. "Wait until you see the Beaulieu Chutes," they said. "They're *complètement magnifiques.*"

After talking to the hikers, I felt far better about being there. It was a little unnerving being alone out there, but at least I knew the trail was finished.

The St. Lawrence River

Reaching the summit of Mont Blanc at sunset, I saw a band of shimmering blue on the horizon. This was the St. Lawrence River, and seeing it was a major milestone. After heading north for hundreds of kilometres, this is where the IAT swings east and heads towards Cap Gaspé and the end of the trail.

Nearly 1,200 kilometres long, the St. Lawrence River starts in the Great Lakes, flows past Montreal and Quebec City, then dumps into the massive Gulf of St.

Lawrence. Here near the mouth, the river was more like an inland sea, so wide that the distant shore was just a faint smudge.

Pods of belugas frolic in these waters, as do blue, humpback and minke whales. Porpoises, dolphins and seals also live here, as do exotic seabirds like double-crested cormorants, razorbills and black-legged kittiwakes. But it would be a while before I'd be bird-watching on the St. Lawrence. First I had to get through the Matane Reserve.

There was a snug little cabin at the top of Mont Blanc. Inside were several beds, a wood stove and a table with a hiker's logbook on top. Opening it up, I found an entry by Eb "Nimblewill Nomad" Eberhart, the retired optometrist I'd heard about back in Maine, and another by someone named Sridhar "Spider" Ramasami, a computer programmer from Florida.

Both men were hiking the Eastern Continental Trail from north to south (Quebec to Florida), and they'd stayed in this cabin within days of each other. I was eager to read what they'd written to know what lay ahead.

Spider's entry was curt and factual, noting weather patterns and trail conditions. Nimblewill's writing was rambling and poetic, and made frequent references to the grace of God. Neither mentioned anything amiss up ahead. Much relieved, I wrote a few lines in the notebook, then stretched out on the bunk. It had been a gruelling hike up Mont Blanc, and I needed a quick nap.

The cabin was dark and hot when I woke up several hours later. I got up to open the door, glancing at the window as I walked past. Far below, twinkling lights lined the shore of the St. Lawrence. I went outside for a better look, but forgot the lights when I saw the stars. It was as if dark, intricate lace had been stretched across the sky, and light from the other side was shining through the holes. I stood there marvelling at the beauty. To think I'd almost missed all this by whipping myself into a neurotic frenzy.

Nimblewill's Rope

The next morning, a heavy fog blanketed the summit. Groping my way through it, I followed the trail to the edge of the mountain, then descended into a gnarled tuckamore forest.

The word "tuckamore" sounds vaguely magical, but actually refers to trees growing in exposed areas that have been stunted and shaped by wind. Wading through

▲ *Log bridge over the Bealieu River in Quebec's Matane Reserve*

the mist past the tortured trees, it was hard to believe that phantoms weren't afoot.

After the tuckamore forest, the trail cut through a meadow of gigantic ferns, zigzagged up and down for a few kilometres, then came out beside an alpine lake. Skirting the lake, I huffed and puffed over a few more hills, then reached the base of Mont Nicol-Albert.

"Terrifying shudder are the only words I can use to describe my feelings along the trail over Mont Nicol-Albert," Nimblewill had written in his journal back in 1998, during his first IAT hike. He'd posted his journal on the internet, where I'd read it before leaving.

> "At one point, I saw a rope tied between two trees ... When I got closer, I stood there in absolute shock. There was nothing below for a thousand feet. Gripping the rope, I peered down into a narrow, vertical-walled chasm. It was as if I was hanging from the sky, perhaps even in flight ..."

◄ *The magnificent Chutes Hélène*

▲ *Woodpecker*

I found Nimblewill's rope, peered expectantly over the cliff, then stepped back completely unimpressed. I haven't seen many yawning chasms in my hiking career (exactly one, and it was only a few feet away), but it didn't look that scary to me. I sidled past the chasm, then picked my way down the steep, narrow path to the top of the Beaulieu Chutes.

Then I saw another yellow rope, then another and another.

The Beaulieu Chutes

The Beaulieu Chutes were a series of waterfalls that tumbled down a steep, narrow gorge. It was almost dark when I got there, so I decided to camp for the night and head down the falls in the morning.

I'm glad I did, because it took three hours to climb down the Beaulieu Chutes the next day. Actually, "climb" is the wrong word. It was more like an endless careening slide down a slick, muddy path, often swinging so close to the edge I nearly pitched into the boiling waters below. Yellow rope had been strung in particularly treacherous places to prevent hikers from going too close to the edge. But those ropes acted like flashing neon signs: "LOOK OVER HERE!" These were usually the best places to view the bubbling, tumbling, shooting, raging chaos below.

After the waterfalls, the trail ran along a road for a few kilometres, then headed into the woods again. I reached Chutes Hélène a few hours later. Visible from almost a kilometre away, this waterfall tumbled off a 70-metre cliff into a clear pool, creating shimmering rainbows in the mist.

Grandfather's Spectacles

I camped a few kilometres from Chutes Hélène that night, then set off for Mont Collins the next morning.

The trail up the mountain was gentle at first, then headed straight uphill. Clinging to bushes and grabbing for rocks, I slowly inched my way up. Trees gave way to tundra, tundra gave way to rocks, but still the trail went up and up. Near the top, I spotted a tiny hunched figure, moving slowly across the far-off saddle between Mont Collins and Mont Matawees.

It looked like a hiker, but for some reason, he was walking doubled over from the waist. I didn't understand why until I clawed my way to the summit. The wind was howling up there. Standing upright was a challenge, but moving forward was a major achievement. Everything seemed in motion. Mountains lumbered off in all directions. Clouds scurried across the sun, flinging curtains of shadow across the landscape, then racing off again, leaving luminous swathes of green.

There was no trail across the fragile alpine tundra, only a series of rocky cairns to mark the way. Some optimistic soul had jammed an IAT signpost into a pile of rocks, but the sign was hanging at a crazy angle, swinging and bobbing in the wind.

I passed the hiker near Mont Matawees. An older gentleman, he reported seeing caribou at the top of Mont Logan, then wished me good day and continued down the path towards Mont Collins.

I lingered for a while in the wide, treeless saddle between Mont Collins and Mont Matawees. Mountains dropped away on both sides of the path, and to the north, the St. Lawrence River rushed towards the sea. The air was so clear that looking out over the mountains was like peering through your grandfather's spectacles as a kid: everything looked too clear, too sharp, too colourful.

I couldn't decide whether this was the most beautiful place I'd ever seen, or if four weeks of walking towards it had made it so. Pondering this, I crossed the saddle and started climbing Mont Matawees.

Mont Matawees

Within seconds, panic shoved beauty aside in my thoughts. The path hugged the edge of a sheer cliff and was so narrow that if a person were to approach from the opposite direction, someone would have to back up. Walking forward on the path was terrifying, but backing up was inconceivable.

Wind screamed up the mountain, flattening me against the rocks. Fear, thick as caramel, raced through my veins. "Don't look down, don't look down, don't look down," I muttered, inching down the path. Midway across, I was seized by the insane desire to take a picture. Taking out my camera, I attached it to a tripod, then tried taking a shot, but the legs wouldn't stop dancing in the wind. I took the picture anyway, praying it was in focus.

Wind-battered spruce tree in Quebec's Matane Reserve ▶

Finally the trail led to a small clump of trees. I dove inside, grateful for a reprieve from the wind. Then I followed the trail as it dropped into a silent valley, crossed a field of boulders and started up the mountain on the other side. Part way up the hill I passed a small sign: "Welcome to the Parc de la Gaspésie."

I had done it. I had survived the Matane Reserve.

"Ah, no big deal," I muttered, and kept on climbing. And remarkably, it hadn't been. It had taken me four days to cross the reserve. Despite the dire warnings, I hadn't gotten lost. And despite not carrying a hunting vest, I hadn't been shot. Instead, I'd seen some truly spectacular country, and it looked even better ahead.

It was a steep, rocky scramble up Mont Fortin. From the summit, the trail ran along a narrow ridge across to Mont Logan. There was a large overnight cabin at the summit. I decided to stay there for the night, even though it was only mid-afternoon. It would be several days before I'd be this high again, and not just in altitude, either. I didn't want one of the most remarkable days of my life to end.

The Parc de la Gaspésie

The cabin on Mont Logan was one of several overnight shelters in the park. The cabins (called *refuges*) are spaced within an easy day's hike of each other, and cost $18 per night. Actually, the *refuges* cost money if you enter the park from the main gates. There'd only been a sign poked into the dirt where I'd entered the park, so there'd been no one to pay. I'd be lying if I said that bothered me.

It was pitch dark when I got up the next morning. Putting on every scrap of clothing in my backpack, I went outside to wait for the sunrise. From here, the sun would rise straight out of the St. Lawrence River, something I'd been looking forward to for weeks.

The sunrise was spectacular — but not nearly as impressive as the caribou. They stole towards the summit, silent as ghosts, and began feeding a short distance away. I dared not move, lest they slip away as silently as they'd come.

I managed to sit still for twenty minutes, then uncontrollable shivering got the better of me. I leapt up, scattering the caribou, and made a dash for the *refuge*. Coffee!

Two other hikers had stayed in the cabin the previous night. They'd gotten in late, so I hadn't spoken to them yet. A fit-looking couple in their forties, they'd already eaten breakfast and were packing their gear when I came back inside.

The couple had hiked the same trail as I had yesterday, and were returning the same way today.

"That bit across Mont Matawees, wasn't that terrifying?" I said to the small but powerful-looking woman.

"What bit?" she asked.

What bit? We were speaking in French. Maybe I'd missed something.

"You know, that bit where it's really steep, and the trail's about three inches wide, and if you slipped and fell, you'd die," I persisted.

"Where exactly?" she asked.

Mont Matawees hadn't bothered that pint-sized woman a bit. This meant that either she was a daredevil, or I was a coward. While I hated to admit it (especially to someone wearing pink nail polish), I suspect the latter.

By the time I got the coffee on, the couple was heading out the door. "Oh, wait," the woman said. Dropping her pack, she rummaged through it, then pulled out a map.

"Here, you can have this," she said. "It's a map of the Parc de la Gaspésie. We have an extra one."

This was more than trail magic. This was scary. I'd just been wondering how I was going to get through the park without a map. The gods weren't just smiling down at me, they were dumping things out of the sky.

I pored over the map for most of the morning. From Mont Logan, the trail ran across some steeply bunched mountains, then descended to a long, skinny lake. From the lake, the trail climbed over a series of smaller peaks, then rose to Mont Albert, a massive mountain topped by a saucer-shaped plateau. From there, it was all downhill to the road and the Gîte du Mont Albert.

I figured it would take me four days to get to the Gîte. There were *refuges* all along the way. One of these, called Le Carouge, was only a few kilometres away.

A Zen Moose Experience

The Carouge cabin looked straight out of a back-to-the-land novel. Built on a small lake, this rustic cabin contained a wood stove and eight bunk beds. I left my

▲ *The Serpentine Trail in Parc de la Gaspésie*

An aerial view of Pic du Brûlé ▶

pack in the cabin and headed for the water. A few minutes later, I was floating on my back in the middle of the lake.

After a short swim, I fell asleep on the dock. I woke up shivering when clouds started drifting across the sun.

I went back up to the cabin to warm up, settling in a chair by the unlit stove. I didn't have a book, so I couldn't read. I wasn't hungry, so I couldn't eat. I'd just woken up, so I couldn't take a nap. And after walking for six weeks straight, I certainly wasn't going for a stroll. So I just sat there, staring at the wall. I didn't have a single thought in my head.

Zen masters spend years trying to achieve an egoless state, but I'm not sure why. Not thinking about anything is an extremely weird sensation. I sat there, blank and unmoving, until darkness fell. Then, finally, I had something to do.

I stood up to make a fire, glancing out the window as I rose. There was a moose, standing in the lake, about twenty metres away. I started a fire, then walked slowly down to the water. The moose didn't notice me. He was too busy dunking his head in the water and gorging on the slime at the bottom of the lake. I walked closer and closer, then I must have crossed some invisible line, because he jerked his head out of the water, scattering slime in all directions, and glared at me suspiciously.

I froze. The moose stared at me for awhile, then ducked his head and started eating again. I stood there, wrapped in the quiet evening, watching the massive animal feed in the fading golden light.

I fell asleep thinking I'd learned something profound that day, but I wasn't sure what it was.

De-clawed Wilderness

The trail was perfect the next day. There were plenty of trail markers and distance signs. The grade of the path was so gradual, it made climbing the mountains seem effortless. There were cute little bridges over boggy patches. In short, every effort had been made to give park visitors an unforgettable wilderness experience. And indeed, the park was spectacular. So why did it seem so tame?

In the Matane Reserve, the wilderness had seemed wild, uncontrolled and completely oblivious to my presence. Here, with the signs and fences, the benches and bridges, the wilderness felt de-clawed, like a slumbering grizzly bear trapped in a zoo. I can't say I minded the peaceful stroll to the next cabin, though.

I stayed at the Huard *refuge* that night, then set off for Lac Cascapédia the next morning.

De-clawed or not, the trail was magnificent. The Appalachians rose out of the St. Lawrence River like a giant cockscomb. I followed the trail along the edge of the headland, a line of wind-battered trees to my right, a sheer drop to my left.

I passed a sign indicating a seven hundred metre side-trip. I almost didn't take it, worried that I wouldn't make it to Lac Cascapédia before dark. And then there was John Watling's detour rule: "Never take a side-trip if it's over half a kilometre."

John was right about most things, but not this time. At the end of the Pic de l'Aube side-trail, there was a magnificent view of Pic de Brûlé, a mountain so ancient it seemed to be sagging back into the earth like a lump of melting butter. The mountain was wrapped in a dark carpet of spruce trees, and far below, the St. Lawrence River was a shining streak of blue.

The side-trip was so spectacular, I wrote John a note, urging him not to miss it. I stuck the note in a plastic bag, then taped it to a sign on the main trail. I wasn't sure how far behind me he was, but I guessed it was no more than a week.

I reached Lac Cascapédia at sunset. There was a large campsite here, and several spacious *refuges*. There was also a ranger's hut. Had I asked the ranger about campsites, he likely would have found me one, and charged me for the night. So I didn't ask. On the Appalachian Trail, long-distance hikers are usually allowed to pass through parks for free. Because the IAT is new and long-distance hikers are rare, this arrangement doesn't exist yet in the Parc de la Gaspésie. Besides, after three nights of sleeping indoors on soft beds, I'd grown quite fond of *refuges*.

Gremlins

I walked into the emptiest looking *refuge* and put my pack in one of the bedrooms. This cabin seemed far more deluxe than the others I'd seen. First, there were three separate bedrooms rather than the usual dormitory-style bunk beds. It also had comfortable furniture, propane heat and light, even a bathroom with hot running water. Plus, the place was deserted. I couldn't believe my luck.

▲ Split-log footpath in Parc de la Gaspésie

Anse-Blanchette, a restored heritage site in Parc Forillion ▶

I took a long shower, cooked supper in the fully equipped kitchen, then fell asleep feeling blissfully content.

An hour later, I was woken by "BANG, mumble, mumble, mumble, BANG" in the next room. Then CRASH! My door flew open, and I saw the silhouettes of two bulky guys looming in the doorway.

"Hey, who are you?" is what I think they said, though I wasn't sure because they both spoke French with impenetrable Gaspé accents.

A few minutes later, I was drinking a cold beer in the living room with my new fishermen friends. Actually, they were talking, and I was nodding and smiling because I couldn't understand a word. But even without language, it was clear that this was a private cabin, and they weren't sure why I was there. They didn't seem to mind, though.

I finished the beer. Then, nodding and smiling, I backed into the bedroom and closed the door. Then, not knowing what else to do, I went back to bed.

After a sleepless night, I leapt out of bed at 4:30 a.m., convinced that the men would wake up, walk to the ranger's hut, and alert him of the grinning half-wit in their cabin. I threw some clothes on, packed my bag and ran.

The Surprising Mont Albert

Walking up Mont Ells in the gloomy half-light, I comforted myself with the thought that I'd needed an early start. It was almost thirty kilometres to Route 299. If all went well, I could be eating supper in the Gîte by nightfall.

The summit of Mont Ells was a swirling mass of wind and clouds. Trees strained at their roots, as if longing to be airborne. Rain began to fall, a few drops at first, then in torrents. Luckily, there was a *refuge* only a few kilometres away. I sloshed inside, started a fire, then huddled close to the stove for warmth. When the rain stopped an hour later, I started walking again.

The trail zigzagged, backtracked, looped around, then zigzagged some more. Dizzy and disoriented, I had no idea which direction I was heading in. Then, through the trees, I glimpsed something soft and smooth and beige. I wasn't expecting to be impressed. I just wanted to get to the Gîte. But through the dark forest, Mont Albert rose like a gigantic tawny whale.

The trail descended into a steeply wooded valley, then crossed a river. The moment my foot touched the far riverbank, everything changed. There were no trees on the other side, and the path beneath my feet changed from earth to stone. A few moments later, I was on top of Mont Albert.

Wind whistled across the summit, smelling of long-buried secrets. I passed two caribou huddled in the lee of a rocky bluff, a carpet of strange white flowers, a small alpine lake. Then I saw more caribou, off in the distance, and more lakes, dark jewels scattered across the barren landscape.

Then, without any warning, the front of the mountain collapsed sheer away and the trail headed straight down. Russet-coloured mountains rose out of the valley, covered at the base by creeping forest. I picked my way down the rocky path, then followed the trail down the valley.

A few hours later, I passed a sign: "Gîte du Mont Albert: 3 kilometres." Then I saw a small red roof through the trees. Could that be it? Over the past few weeks, the Gîte had grown into a full-sized utopia. This didn't look good. I quickly began whittling down my expectations.

Then, finally, I was standing on the road. To most people, this was just Route 299. But to me, that dark ribbon of concrete was a wondrous sight. I had done it. I was very proud of getting through the Matane Reserve and the Parc de la Gaspésie. Not because it was difficult — it wasn't — but because I'd wrestled my fear to the ground and pummelled it into oblivion.

The Gîte was less than a kilometre away. It didn't matter that the place was probably no bigger than a doghouse. Heading down the road, I felt a foolish grin spread across my face.

The Doghouse

The road curved to the left, revealing a turret. Then more turrets popped into view. Soon I was standing in front of what looked like a massive Bavarian castle. The grin faded. My jaw dropped.

I walked into the Gîte du Mont Albert covered in eight days of trail dust, smelling like a wet dog, my hair a suspicious lump under my hat. The staff didn't bat an eye. They acted as if I was clad in taffeta and diamonds, and told me that dinner was at eight o'clock. I wandered into the dining room, ordered a drink and looked around.

While daydreaming about the Gîte, I hadn't thought to picture the dining room. Massive chandeliers hung from the ceiling. A moose head brooded above the stone fireplace, resentful perhaps that the starched tablecloths, winking oil lamps and sparking crystal would be forever out of reach.

Dinner was even better than I had imagined: smoked salmon with strawberries and capers, frog's-leg chowder garnished with a floating nasturtium leaf ("Careful, there might be a frog underneath that lily pad," the waitress joked), followed by rack of lamb, new potatoes dusted with paprika, grilled tomatoes and long elegant curls of zucchini.

I sat alone in the dining room, eating my way through an elaborate seven-course dinner. Surprisingly, it was a bittersweet experience. Food tastes better when shared with another, and I had no one to share it with.

Last Leg

My trip ended — spiritually at least — the moment I reached the Gîte du Mont Albert. From here, the IAT continues east through the park, then cuts across to the north coast of the Gaspé. The trail follows the road for five days, then crosses into Parc Forillon. From there, it's a two-day walk to Cap Gaspé, where the IAT ends with a dramatic flourish at the tip of a rocky promenade.

By the time I finished eating, I'd made my decision. My trip was over, but I wanted to hike the last section of the IAT through Parc Forillon, so I could finish my trip at Cap Gaspé.

There was an information centre just down the road from the Gîte. From there, I could catch a shuttle to the main road, where buses leave daily for Forillon Park. I bought a ticket, got a take-out coffee, then sat under a tree to wait for the bus.

I'd barely taken a sip of my coffee when a familiar figure strode by. John Watling! The

▲ *Tail flukes of a humpback, one of three species of baleen whales that live in the St. Lawrence River*

The silhouette known as Le Vieux *(the old man), in the cliff at* Cap Gaspé ▲

last time I'd seen him was in Nictau, New Brunswick. I couldn't believe he'd caught up to me. With all the hitchhiking I'd done, he should have been several days behind.

"John!" I yelled, racing across the grass.

He stopped, tried smiling, but the effort seemed too great. He stood there, face pinched with pain, trying to look happy to see me.

"My god, what's the matter?"

"Ran out of food in the Matane Reserve," he said. "Got through the reserve and the Parc de la Gaspésie in four and a half days. I'm exhausted. My feet are a mess."

It had taken me eight days to cover the same distance. When I pointed this out to him, he shrugged modestly, then perked up a bit.

It was great seeing each other again. I asked if he'd gotten lost in the dreaded Restigouche section (he had), and whether he'd taken the Pic de l'Aube side-trail (he hadn't). He looked slightly puzzled when I told him how worried I'd been about hiking through the Matane Reserve. But despite his exhaustion and my paranoia, we agreed it had been the high point of our trip.

Waving goodbye to John a second time, I knew I'd made a friend for life. After a short break, John headed east through the park on the IAT. I watched his blue knapsack until it disappeared, then got on the bus and headed for Parc Forillon.

I picked up the IAT at the western end of the park. I covered ten kilometres by nightfall, then camped beside a stream. This was my last night on the IAT. To celebrate, I ate a double helping of instant noodles and turned in early.

It was so cold the next morning, I half expected to see snowdrifts when I zipped open the tent. There was no snow, but a silver mantle of frost was draped over the tent. I packed up quickly, glad to be almost finished, and headed down the trail.

The path ran through forest for most of the morning, then slowly started to climb. From the top of Mont Saint-Alban, there was a panoramic view of Baie des Chaleurs, the body of water off the south coast of the Gaspé Peninsula. Boats zipped across the shining water, tiny as water beetles. These craft were real, though I wished one was the famous phantom. Seeing the burning ghost ship of the Baie des Chaleurs would have been a great way to end my IAT hike.

Over the years, there have been countless sightings of a flaming three-masted schooner on the Baie des Chaleurs. Some people reported seeing a burning ship manned by sailors in blue uniforms. Others have seen men running on the deck of the burning ship, with a woman standing in front with extended arms. Still others saw a burning ship with no one aboard at all. While accounts vary, most agree that seeing the burning ghost ship is unlucky. Maybe it's just as well I didn't see it.

The path headed down the hill, then came out beside the sea. My steps quickened. From here, it was less than five kilometres to the end of the IAT.

The trail ran along the rocky coastline, past crumbling graves filled with the tired bones of Guernsey fishermen, past fields of waving fireweed, past the colourful remains of an old movie set (as if throwing up a few hollow buildings, draping a net over the fence and artfully placing a few rosy-cheeked fishermen could capture the harsh life of the sea). It continued across a pebbly beach where the incoming tide nipped at my boots, through a dark patch of forest, past a lonely house perched on a cliff and up a long hill. Then, suddenly, I was at the tip of the Gaspé Peninsula, surrounded by shimmering sea.

I could say that I gazed into the infinite ocean, flooded by a sense of personal accomplishment, or that I thought about Dick Anderson and his inspiring dream of building an international trail, or that I stood there, humbled by the dedication of the volunteers who'd turned Dick's dream into reality.

I did think these things, but not then. At that moment, I was thinking about the book I would write, wondering how I was going to squeeze seven weeks of adventure, ecstasy and fear into a mere 137 pages.

Shimmering surf in Quebec's Parc Forillon ▶

The Essential Guide

Table of Contents

T he Essential Guide is exactly what it says it is — essential. It will be your constant companion, both in planning your IAT hike and out on the trail.

The Essential Guide was designed to be used with official IAT hiking guides. There are three IAT guides available: Maine, New Brunswick and Quebec (ordering info page 144). These guides are invaluable for up-to-date trail information, but they don't include things like transportation to the IAT trailheads, where to order maps, post office addresses and opening hours, IAT trail friends, park addresses, towns with internet access, locations of medical clinics, etc. These services (and many others) are all included in this guide.

In short, use the IAT hiking guides for up-to-date trail information, but use the Essential Guide for everything else — even planning your trip.

Note that all prices are in Canadian dollars, unless otherwise specified. Also note that distances are in kilometres, except for the Maine section, where miles appear first, followed by kilometres in parentheses.

Trip Planner

Fill in the Trip Planner six months before your IAT hike. Write your departure date at the top of the chart, then fill in the dates below. For example, if your departure date is July 15, write "March 15" next to *"4 months before,"* "April 15" next to *"3 months before,"* and so on. As each date arrives, do the suggested tasks.

DEPARTURE DATE:_____

MONTH	DATE	TASK	PAGE
By January 15th of the year you intend to hike the IAT		Make Baxter State Park reservations	146
4 months before		Start background reading	170
3 months before		Buy, organize and test gear	150
2 months before		Organize maps and IAT hiking guides	144
1 month before		Book transportation to the IAT	143
2 weeks before		Mail food to post offices	148
1 week before		Contact the IAT with your itinerary	146

Preparing to Hike the International Appalachian Trail

WHICH DIRECTION SHOULD YOU GO?

The International Appalachian Trail goes from Mount Katahdin, Maine to Cap Gaspé, Quebec, a distance of over 1,000 kilometres (600 miles). While the trail can be hiked in either direction, it's preferable to travel from **Maine to Gaspé**. This allows you to start your trek with a spectacular four-day hike from the IAT trailhead on Mount Katahdin's windy summit (one vertical mile straight up), then north through Baxter State Park.

Baxter State Park is one of New England's most popular hiking destinations. Because the park is so popular, campsite reservations must be made months in advance. With campsite reservations, however, hiking dates through the park become fixed. Hiking from Gaspé to Maine, it's virtually impossible to know exactly what date you'll arrive at Baxter Park — which is why it's preferable to hike from Maine to Gaspé.

Even without reservations, it's still possible to hike the IAT from Maine to Gaspé. For this option, you can buy a day pass to hike up Mount Katahdin, then follow the road to Millinocket and beyond (see page 152 for details).

Another excellent reason for hiking the IAT from Maine to Gaspé is that the terrain in Maine and New Brunswick is relatively easy (mostly country roads and converted rail/trails), while the trail in Quebec is far more challenging. By starting in Maine, you can spend a few weeks getting in shape before hitting Quebec's Shickshock Mountains — which the locals call the "Rockies of the East" for good reason.

Even though this guide is arranged from Maine to Gaspé, it can be followed in reverse for hikers travelling from **Gaspé to Maine**. The best reason for hiking the IAT in this direction is that you get to see the most scenic part of the trail first.

In Quebec, IAT hikers experience everything from rugged mountains to fragile tundra, from tumbling waterfalls to wind-lashed sea. But while the scenery in Quebec is spectacular, it's the variety and abundance of wildlife that makes hiking in this province exceptional. In addition to the usual array of wild critters, Canada's southernmost caribou herd lives in Quebec, atop the Shickshock Mountains, a remote and secret world of alpine wildflowers, blue and scarlet berries, and ancient, pockmarked boulders. The IAT also follows the St. Lawrence River for several days. Pods of belugas frolic in these shimmering waters, as do blue, humpback and minke whales. Porpoises, dolphins and seals also live here, as do exotic seabirds such as double-crested cormorants, razorbills and black-legged kittiwakes.

The IAT is so impressive in Quebec that hard-core hikers might be tempted to skip Maine and New Brunswick and head straight for *la belle province*. But what Maine and New Brunswick lack in scenery, they make up for in folksy, down-home charm: old men roll beside you in their cars as you're walking down the road; farmers' wives invite you in for supper; people offer you places to stay, things to wear, the use of their showers, canoe rides — even farm animals. "Why carry that dratted thing when my mule could do it for you?" someone asked me during my hike.

The IAT is really two trails, then. The path through Maine and New Brunswick allows the hiker to experience the kindness and generosity that still exists in rural North America, while the trail in Quebec wends its way through some truly spectacular scenery.

GETTING TO THE TRAILHEAD

Hiking South to North

From Canada: Woodstock, New Brunswick, is the closest Canadian town to the IAT trailhead in Baxter State Park. From Woodstock, take a taxi to Houlton, Maine (Don's Taxi). From Houlton, take a bus to Medway (Cyr Bus Lines). From Medway, take a taxi to Baxter State Park's Katahdin Stream Campground (Katahdin Taxi).

From the USA: Boston, Massachusetts, is the closest major city to the IAT trailhead in Baxter State Park. From Boston, take a bus to Bangor, Maine (Greyhound USA). From Bangor, transfer to the local bus company and travel to Medway (Cyr Bus Lines). From Medway, take a taxi to Baxter State Park's Katahdin Stream Campground (Katahdin Taxi).

Hiking North to South

From Canada or the USA: Gaspé is the closest town to the IAT trailhead in Forillon National Park. From the town of Gaspé, take a taxi to Parc Forillon's Cap-Bon-Ami Campground (Kennedy Taxi). If travelling by bus, IAT hikers can get off at Cap-aux-Os, then road walk 2 km to Forillon National Park. After entering the park, it's another 6 km to Cap-Bon-Ami Campground. NOTE: For those who want a good night's sleep before hitting the trail, there's an International Youth Hostel in Cap-aux-Os (tel: 418-892-5153).

BUS

COMPANY	INTERNET	PHONE NUMBER
Greyhound USA	www.greyhound.com	1-800-229-9494
Greyhound Canada	www.greyhound.ca	1-800-661-8747
Cyr Bus Lines (Maine)	www.cyrbustours.com	1-800-244-2335; 207-827-2335

COMPANY	INTERNET	PHONE NUMBER
SMT Bus Lines (N.B.)	www.smtbus.com	1-800-567-5151; 506-859-5100
Orleans Express (Quebec)	www.orleansexpress.com	1-888-999-3977; 514-395-4000
Montreal Bus Station		514-842-2281
Gaspé Bus Station		418-368-1888

TRAIN

COMPANY	INTERNET	PHONE NUMBER
Amtrak (USA)	www.amtrak.com	1-800-USA-RAIL
VIA Rail (Canada)	www.viarail.ca	1-888-VIA-RAIL

TAXI

COMPANY	FROM/TO	COST	PHONE NUMBER
Katahdin Taxi	From Medway, ME to Baxter State Park	$US 45	207-723-2000
Don's Taxi	From Woodstock, N.B. to Houlton, ME	$CAN 25	506-325-9700
Kennedy Taxi	From Gaspé, Que. to Forillon National Park	$CAN 35	418-368-2137

IAT HIKING GUIDES

To obtain IAT hiking guides for Maine, New Brunswick and Quebec, either download them from the IAT's website, or contact each of the separate IAT sections (IAT contact info page 147).

MAPS

MAINE

IAT **Map (Maine):** Download IAT Maine's one-page map from the IAT website (website info page 147). While this map gives a good overview of the IAT in Maine, it's too small for practical purposes. Instead of taking it on the trail, transfer the route onto a detailed road map. The 1:125,000 topographic maps in DeLorme's *Maine Atlas and Gazetteer* are excellent, but any road map will do.

Baxter State Park Hiking Maps: Maps of the park are available on the internet, but are difficult to read. Order maps directly from the park (Baxter State Park contact info page 146).

NEW BRUNSWICK

IAT **Map (New Brunswick):** Download the IAT New Brunswick maps from the IAT website (website info page 147). Despite their marginal quality, plan to take these maps with you. For back-up, draw the IAT onto a detailed road map. For a free road map, call Tourism New Brunswick (1-800-561-0123).

Mount Carleton Hiking Maps: Order maps from Mount Carleton Provincial Park before you go, or pick them up when you arrive (Mount Carleton contact info page 146).

Restigouche River Maps: If you choose to canoe the Restigouche River, Arpin Canoe Restigouche sells maps at a reasonable cost (Arpin Canoe contact info page 146).

QUEBEC

IAT **Maps (Quebec):** The following maps are available from IAT Quebec for $7.50 each: "Matapédia Valley," "Matane Wildlife Reserve," "Upper Gaspé" and "Gaspé Coast Sector" (IAT Quebec contact info page 147).

Parc de la Gaspésie Hiking Maps: Call the park and order their recently updated 1:75,000 topographic map ($5.00), and their free IAT map (Parc de la Gaspésie contact info page 146).

Forillon National Park Hiking Maps: Call Forillon National Park and order "The Trails of Forillon National Park" map ($2.00) and a free "Forillon National Park Visitor's Guide" (Forillon National Park contact info page 146).

PARKS

MAINE

Baxter State Park (with campsite reservations):

With pre-booked campsite reservations in Baxter State Park, people can start the IAT with a four-day hike through the park. For this option, **campsite reservations must be made by**

January 15th of the year you intend to travel. Baxter State Park begins taking reservations — by mail and in person only — on the first business day in January. The best campsites are sold out in the first few weeks, while everything else is booked by March.

There are many routes through Baxter State Park. Either follow the suggested itinerary or plan your own. Be aware that the park does not recommend that hikers travel more than 10 miles (16 km) per day.

Suggested itinerary:

Night 1: Camp at Roaring Brook campsite. The next day, hike to the top of Katahdin, then return to Roaring Brook Campsite for the night.

Night 2: Camp at Roaring Brook campsite. The next day, hike to Russell Pond campsite.

Night 3: Camp at Russell Pond campsite. The next day, hike as far as South Branch Pond campsite.

Night 4: Camp at South Branch Pond campsite. The next day, leave Baxter State Park through Matagammon Gate, then walk east on Grand Lake Road.

Baxter State Park (without campsite reservations):

Without pre-booked campsite reservations, it is virtually impossible to start your IAT hike with a four-day hike through Baxter State Park. Instead, you may choose to start the IAT with a day hike up Mount Katahdin.

For this option, purchase a day pass at the park's south entrance (Togue Pond Gate). **Arrive no later than 5:00 a.m., as day passes are distributed on a first-come, first-served basis**. Once the park's daily allotment of passes are sold, the entrance gate closes for the day. After buying your pass, go to Katahdin Stream Campground. To avoid carrying your pack up the mountain, ask if you can leave it at Katahdin Stream ranger station (the ranger usually has day packs to borrow as well). From Katahdin Stream Campground, follow the Hunt Trail to Mount Katahdin summit.

NEW BRUNSWICK

Mount Carleton Provincial Park: IAT hikers do not require campsite reservations for this park.

QUEBEC

SEPAQ: Many of the campsites and *refuges* (dormitory-style overnight cabins) along the IAT in Quebec are administered by SEPAQ (Société des Etablissements de Plein Air du Québec). The campsites cost $7 per tent per night, while *refuges* cost $15 per night. All SEPAQ accommodations are listed in the Quick-Look Chart (page 164). (SEPAQ contact info page 146).

Réserve Faunique de Matane (Matane Reserve): Hikers must reserve campsites and *refuges* before travelling through the reserve. Bookings can be made in advance by calling SEPAQ, or in person when you enter the reserve.

NOTE: Hunting is allowed during the fall in the Matane Reserve. As a result, IAT **hikers face certain restrictions if hiking through the Matane Reserve during hunting season** (limited daily hiking hours, orange hiking vests recommended). Hunting season varies from year to year, but usually starts in early September. If you're planning to be in the Matane Reserve at this time, call Poste John in the reserve and ask when hunting season starts (Poste John contact info this page).

Parc de la Gaspésie: Hikers must reserve campsites and *refuges* before travelling through the Parc de la Gaspésie. Since there is no park office when you cross the western perimeter of the park on the IAT, reservations should be made when entering the Matane Reserve.

Forillon National Park: No reservations required. Camping at backcountry sites is free.

PARK ADDRESSES

Baxter State Park (Maine)
64 Balsam Drive
Millinocket, ME
04462
Tel: 207-723-5140
Internet: www.baxterstateparkauthority.com

SEPAQ (Quebec)
One number for all campsite, shelter and *refuge* reservations
Tel: 1-800-665-6527
Internet: www.SEPAQ.com

Parc de la Gaspésie (Quebec)
Route 299, C.P. 299
Sainte-Anne-des-Monts, Quebec
G0E 2G0
Tel: 888-783-2663
Internet: www.SEPAQ.com

Restigouche River (by canoe)
Arpin Canoe Restigouche
8 Chemin Arpin
Kedgwick River, N.B.
E8B 1R9
1-877-259-4440; 506-284-3140

Mount Carleton Provincial Park (New Brunswick)
11 Gagnon St.
Saint-Quentin, N.B.
E8A 1N4
Tel: 506-235-0793
Internet: www.gov.nb.ca/0078/carleton/index.htm

Matane Reserve (Quebec)
257 rue Saint-Jérôme
Matane, Québec
G4W 3A7
Tel: 418-224-3345 (Poste John)
Internet: www.SEPAQ.com

Forillon National Park (Quebec)
122 Gaspé Boulevard
Gaspé, Quebec
G4X 1A9
Tel: 418-368-5505
Internet: www.parkscanada.pch.gc.ca/forillon/

OFFICIAL IAT CONTACTS

While it's not required, the IAT asks that hikers submit their travel itinerary to one of the official IAT contacts before leaving on their hike (approximate dates are fine). They also encourage hikers to check in with IAT trail friends along the way.

IAT MAINE	IAT NEW BRUNSWICK	IAT QUEBEC
Dick Anderson	Bob Melville	Viateur De Champlain
27 Flying Point Road	34 Adams St.	616 St. Redempteur
Freeport, Maine 04032	Tide Head, N.B. E3N 4T3	Matane, Quebec G4W 1L1
Tel: 207-865-6233	Tel: 506-753-5789	Tel: 418-562-1240, ext. 2299
E-mail: richardban@iopener.net	E-mail: melvilla@nbnet.nb.ca	E-mail: sia-iat@sia-iat.com

International Appalachian Trail Website: www.internationalat.org

IAT TRAIL FRIENDS

Contact the people listed below for IAT trail info, for local sight-seeing info, to sign an IAT trail registry, or just to see a friendly face.

MAINE:

LOCATION	NAME	NOTES	PHONE NUMBER
Medway	Mike Boutin	Owner, Pinegrove Campground	207-746-5172
Ludlow Road	John Camilleri ("Johnny Down Under")	To meet this gentle, cave-dwelling hermit, look for green mailbox about 1 mile east on Ludlow Road from Ludlow Town Line Road.	No phone
Bridgewater	Mr. Eric Finnamore	Ask this talkative old-timer for a tour of "world's highest" outhouse.	207-429-9520

NEW BRUNSWICK:

LOCATION	NAME	NOTES	PHONE NUMBER
Arthurette	Cathy Sullivan	Cathy invites IAT hikers to stop and sign her IAT trail registry at her white house near the Wagon Wheel restaurant.	506-273-2756
Plaster Rock	Tom Chamberlain	Owner of Tobique View Motel	506-356-2683
Riley Brook	Paul and Lucie McGuinness	Helpful owners of Riley Brook General Store. Don't forget to sign Lucie's trail registry.	506-356-2548
Nictau	Bill Miller	World's friendliest canoe-builder.	506-356-2409
Kedgwick	Maurice Simon	Very knowledgeable about Restigouche Section. IAT goes right past his front door. Watch for beige house with burgundy roof before entering town.	506-284-9194

QUEBEC:

LOCATION	NAME	NOTES	PHONE NUMBER
Matapédia	David LeBlanc	Be sure to contact David before leaving town, as some sections of Matapédia Valley are confusing.	418-865-2100

MAILING SUPPLY BOXES

Hikers have two options with food on the trail: you can either mail supply boxes to post offices along the IAT, or buy food as you go. Mailing supply boxes before leaving is a much better option (better food, more variety, cheaper), but it does require significant planning. Regardless of which option you choose, remember that a long-distance hiker's diet should consist of 70 percent carbohydrates (grains, vegetables and legumes), 15 percent protein and 15 percent fat. For more information, consult Fleming's *The Well-Fed Backpacker* (see Suggested Reading page 170 for details).

POST OFFICES

United States: U.S. post offices will hold packages mailed to General Delivery for up to one month. Packages can also be forwarded from post office to post office within the U.S. at no extra cost.

Canada: In Canada, only certain post offices have General Delivery service. Call the post offices in the towns where you'd like to receive packages to be sure it's allowed. Also note that in Canada, packages must be addressed to the post office's street address.

Mailing packages across the U.S./Canada border: When mailing packages internationally, the contents of each parcel must be listed on a customs form (available at all post offices). Be specific when listing contents (three pairs of socks, 12 granola bars, one pair of boot laces, etc.). The more accurate you are, the less chance your packages will be delayed by a customs inspection.

HOW TO ADDRESS PACKAGES:

IN U.S.A.	IN CANADA
Hiker's Name	Hiker's Name
c/o General Delivery	c/o Poste Restante
Town, State	Town, Province
USA	Canada
Zip Code	Postal Code
"Please hold for IAT hiker"	"S. V. P. gardez pour SIA randonneur."

MAINE:

TOWN	ZIP CODE	HOURS OF OPERATION	PHONE NUMBER
Millinocket	04462	M–F: 8:15–4:45, Sat: 8:15–12:00	207-723-5921
Patten	04765	M–F: 9:00–4:00 (closed 11:30–12:30) Sat: 9:00–12:00	207-528-2210
Smyrna Mills	04780	M–F: 7:30–4:30 (closed 12:00–1:00) Sat: 7:30–11:30	207-757-8241
Houlton	04730	M–F: 8:00–5:00, Sat: 8:00–12:00	207-532-3506
Monticello	04760	M–F: 8:00–4:00 (closed from 12:15–1:15) Sat: 8:00–11:00	207-538-9741
Bridgewater	04735	M–F: 8:00–12:00, 2:00–5:00, Sat: 8:00–11:00	207-429-8259
Mars Hill	04758	M–F: 8:00–4:45, Sat: 8:00–11:30	207-429-9177

NEW BRUNSWICK:

TOWN	ADDRESS	HOURS OF OPERATION	PHONE NUMBER
Perth-Andover	580 East Riverside (Perth side) E7H 1Z4	M–F: 8:30–5:00 Sat: 9:00–12:30	506-273-2890
Plaster Rock	62 Orange St. E7G 1W0	M–F: 8:00–5:00, Sat: 9:00–1:00	506-356-2689
Kedgwick	25 rue Notre-Dame E8B 1R0	M–F: 8:30–5:00, Sat: 10:00–1:00	506-284-2178

QUEBEC: Very few postal workers speak English in this region of Quebec. If you can't speak French, postal codes and street addresses can be verified on the internet (www.canadapost.com)

TOWN	ADDRESS	HOURS OF OPERATION	PHONE NUMBER
Matapédia	3 Macdonell St. G0J 1V0	M–F: 9:00–12:30, 1:30–5:50 Sat: 9:00–11:45	418-865-2188
Causapscal	480 rue Saint-Jacques Nord G0J 1J0	M–F: 8:30–5:30 Sat: 9:00–12:00	418-756-3869
Saint-Alexandre-des-Lacs	16 rue Poirier G0J 2C0	M–F: 9:00–12:00, 3:30–5:30, Sat: 9:00–12:00	418-778-3494
Amqui	10 ave du Parc G0J 1A0	M–F: 8:30–5:15 Sat: closed	418-629-3080
Saint-Vianney	125 ave Centrale G0J 3J0	M–F: 9:00–4:15 Sat: 9:15–12:30	418-629-3705
Cap-Chat	42 rue Notre-Dame G0J 1E0	M–F: 8:30–5:30 Sat: 9:00–11:30	418-786-5920
Saint-Anne-des-Monts	56, 7e rue O G4V 1A0	M–F: 8:15–5:15 Sat: closed	418-763-3411
Mont-Saint-Pierre	104A Prudent-Cloutier G0E 1V0	M–F: 9:00–5:00 Sat: closed	418-797-5160
Madeleine-Centre	117 rue Principale G0E 1P0	M–F: 8:30–8:00 Sat: 3:30–6:00	418-393-2411
Grande-Vallée	7 Saint-François-Xavier Est G0E 1K0	M–F: 8:30–5:00 Sat: 9:00–1:45	418-393-2090
Gaspé	41 blvd. Renaud Est G4X 1S0	M–F: 8:30–5:30 Sat: 9:00–12:00	418-269-3768

HOSPITALS AND CLINICS

MAINE:

TOWN	ADDRESS	PHONE NUMBER
Millinocket	Millinocket Regional Hospital, 200 Somerset St.	207-723-5161
Patten	Katahdin Valley Health Centre, 15 Houlton St.	207-528-2285
Houlton	Houlton Regional Hospital, 20 Hartford St.	207-532-9471
Mars Hill	Aroostook Medical Centre, 140 Academy St.	207-768-4000

NEW BRUNSWICK:	ADDRESS	PHONE NUMBER
Perth-Andover	Hotel Dieu Saint Joseph, 10 Woodland Hill	506-273-7100
Plaster Rock	Tobique Valley Hospital, 120 Main St.	506-356-6600
Campbelltown	Campbelltown Regional Hospital, 189 Lily Lake Rd.	506-789-5000

QUEBEC: All minor medical problems are treated by clinics called CLSCs		PHONE NUMBER
Matapédia	CLSC Malauze, 14 blvd. Perron	418-865-2221
Causapscal	CLSC de la Vallée, 558 rue Saint-Jacques Nord	418-756-3451
Amqui	CLSC de la Vallée, 65 blvd. Saint-Benoît Ouest	418-629-2005
Cap-Chat	CLSC de Cap-Chat, 49 Notre-Dame	418-786-5594
Saint-Anne-des-Monts	CLSC Des Monts, 52 rue Belvédère	418-763-7771
Grande-Vallée	CLSC Mer et Montagnes, 71 Saint-François-Xavier (open 24 hours)	418-393-2572
Rivière-au-Renard	CLSC Mer et Montagnes, 54 blvd. Renard Est	418-269-2572
Gaspé	CLSC Mer et Montagnes, 205 blvd. York Ouest	418-368-2572

HOSPITALS:	ADDRESS	PHONE NUMBER
Amqui	Centre hospitalier d'Amqui, 135 rue de l'Hôpital	418-629-2211
Saint-Anne-des-Monts	Hôpital des Monts, 50 rue Belvédère	418-763-2261
Gaspé	Centre hospitalier de Gaspé, 215 blvd. York Ouest	418-368-3301

EQUIPMENT CHECKLIST

In *The Complete Walker III*, author Colin Fletcher cautions that "Your opinions on equipment and technique must never fossilize into dogma." Mr. Fletcher is absolutely right, except when it comes to weight. Please repeat the following mantra when packing for your IAT hike: "The lighter my pack is, the more I'll enjoy hiking. The heavier my pack is, the more I'll enjoy camping."

PACK	SLEEPING	COOKING/EATING
1 60–80 litre backpack	1 tent	1 backpacking stove with fuel bottle
1 nylon pack cover	1 sleeping bag	1 pot (doubles as bowl)
	1 sleeping pad ★	1 plastic spoon (Lexan)
		1 lighter
		1 large folded sheet of tinfoil (doubles as pot lid and wind screen)

★   Self-inflating mattresses (such as Therm-a-Rest ®) are comfortable, but they're also heavy, expensive and easily damaged (must use a stuff sack and carry a repair kit). While not as luxurious, a closed-cell foam pad might be a better option. Light, cheap and indestructible, these pads can be used on bare ground without fear of damaging them. Whatever you buy, remember that three-quarter-length pads are lighter than full-sized ones.

CLOTHING	FOOTWEAR	FIRST AID
1 pair long pants★★	1 pair hiking boots	Moleskin
1 pair shorts	1 pair sandals or flip-flops	Band-Aids
2 T-shirts		Aspirin
1 long-sleeved shirt★★★		Antiseptic pads (foil-wrapped,
1 fleece jacket		pre-moistened)
1 fleece vest		
1 set of long underwear	**TOILETRIES**	**WAIST CARRY BAG++**
(tops and bottoms)★★★★	Shampoo (travel size, doubles as	Sunscreen+++
1 brightly coloured baseball cap	soap)	Pocket knife++++
(for sun protection and visibility	Toothbrush (travel size)	Lip balm
during hunting season)	Toothpaste (mini tube)	Insect repellent
1 fleece hat (opt.)	Dental floss (doubles as sewing	Sunglasses
3 pairs wool socks	thread; store needle inside con-	Small notebook and pen
3 pairs underwear	tainer)	Money/credit card
1 bandanna	Hand lotion (travel size)	
1 set rain gear (jacket and pants)	Backpacker's towel	
1 pair fleece gloves (opt.)	Mirror (small, folding)	
	Hairbrush/comb	

MISCELLANEOUS

Compass	Headlamp ("Petzl Micro" is	Emergency whistle (hang from
Water bottle with waist belt	excellent)	pack)
carrier	Camera and film	Toilet paper (flatten roll, store in
25 m nylon cord (for repairs,	Journal	a Ziploc bag)
clothesline, etc.)	Important addresses and phone	Thermometer (hang from pack)
Duct tape (small roll, for repairs)	numbers (store in a	Hiking poles (opt.)
3 m wire (for repairs)	Ziploc bag)	
Water purification system+		

★★   Preferably with detachable legs.

★★★   Preferably made from a lightweight, good quality synthetic. Don't be afraid to spend money on this item, as you'll be wearing it every day.

★★★★ Long underwear made from lightweight, good quality synthetics (capilene, polypropylene, etc.) are expensive, but you won't regret this purchase on cold, wet days.

+   Hikers face a dizzying array of options when choosing a water purification system. One popular solution is "Polar Pure," which uses concentrated iodine crystals. Water is safe to drink 20 minutes after treatment.

++   A small waist bag is great for frequently used items such as lip balm, pocket knife, notebook, etc.

+++   Fair-skinned people should use a sunscreen with an SPF of at least 15. Choose a lotion with both UVA and UVB protection. Many sunscreens also contain PABA, but recent studies indicate that PABA could be carcinogenic. For total sun protection, remember the SLIP, SLAP, SLOP rule: SLIP a shirt on, SLAP a hat on, and SLOP on the sunscreen.

++++ While not exactly light, the 4 oz. (114 gram) "Leatherman Mini-Tool ®" is an excellent choice; it comes with pliers, a screwdriver and an optional carry-case.

The Essential Guide
STEP BY STEP

This part of the Essential Guide takes you through every stage of the IAT. Note that all prices in the Maine section are in American dollars, while those in the New Brunswick and Quebec sections are in Canadian dollars. Also note that distances are in kilometres, except for the Maine section, where miles appear first, followed by kilometres in parentheses. Throughout this part of the guide, the names of towns and villages appear in SMALL CAPITALS.

Section One: Maine

Hiking days in Maine: 7–10 days

ACCOMMODATION PRICE GUIDE

\$= US 10–15	\$\$= US 15–20	\$\$\$= US 20–30	\$\$\$\$= US 30–50	\$\$\$\$\$= US 50+

If you have camping reservations in Baxter State Park, follow the "Baxter Park" instructions; if not, follow the "Country Roads" instructions. The "Country Roads" and "Baxter Park" trails meet and become a single trail a few miles south of the Moro Road on Route 11.

"Country Roads" Hike (5–7 days)

Without reserving campsites several months in advance, it's virtually impossible to start your IAT hike with a four-day hike through Baxter State Park (see page 146 for details). Instead, hikers can start with a day hike up Mount Katahdin. After climbing to the summit, follow the Hunt Trail back down to Katahdin Stream Campground (\$), 5.2 miles (8.3 km) away, where lean-tos have been set aside for long-distance hikers on a first-come, first-served basis.

From Katahdin Stream Campground, follow the Appalachian Trail south to Abol Bridge Campground and Store (\$, good supply of hiking food, hot showers, no phone), 9.8 miles (15.7 km) away. From Abol Bridge Campground, there's an old, broken-up blacktop road behind the store (near the gravel pit). Follow this road to Route 157, about 3.8 miles (6 km) away.

From Route 157, it's an 8-mile (12.8-km) road walk to Big Moose Inn, Cabins and Campground (\$ to \$\$\$\$, 207-723-8391, cold beer in lounge, rustic restaurant, swimming in nearby lake, white-water rafting available). Right beside Big Moose is the North Woods

Trading Post (groceries, ATM, camping fuel, pay phone). If you want to stay at the AT Lodge in Millinocket, you can call ahead from here.

From Big Moose Campground, follow Route 157 to Millinocket, 9 miles (14.4 km) away. About a mile before town, you will pass the Hidden Springs Campground ($, 207-723-6337, IAT-friendly owners Michael and Gail Seile).

MILLINOCKET **(downtown):** Post office, Appalachian Trail Lodge ($$$, 207-723-6720, jammed with hiking paraphernalia), Appalachian Trail Café (mom-style cooking; be sure to sign the hiker's registry), laundromat, ATM, Levasseurs Hardware, Millinocket Regional Hospital, Blue Ox Saloon, internet access at Millinocket Memorial Library (5 Maine Ave.) and Mountain Village Café (112 Central St.).

MILLINOCKET **(heading out of town on Route 11):** Best Western Motor Inn, McDonald's, IGA (grocery store), ATM, Rite-Aid Pharmacy.

From Millinocket, follow Route 11 to Pinegrove Campground and Cottages ($ to $$$$$, 207-746-5172, store, laundromat, IAT-friendly owner Mike Boutin), 14 miles (22.4 km) away. From Pinegrove, follow Route 11 for 21 miles (33.6 km) north to Sherman Junction.

SHERMAN JUNCTION: Katahdin Valley Motel ($$$$, 207-365-4554), Sherman Dairy Bar (ice cream, fast-food), Irving Big Stop (restaurant), no pay phone. From Sherman Junction, there are gorgeous views of Mount Katahdin (often mist-shrouded) all the way to Patten, 9 miles (14.4 km) away.

PATTEN: Post office, Patten Motel ($$$$, 207-528-2169), Downtown Deli (village hangout, good food), Pa's Pizza 'n' Sub (pay phone outside), IGA (grocery store), laundromat, ATM, hardware store, pharmacy, medical clinic, internet access at Veterans' Memorial Library (near post office). At the north end of town is Raymond's Clam Shack (don't miss it!) and the Lumberman's Museum (on Route 159, a few hundred metres from the Clam Shack).

From Patten, it's a pleasant road walk on Route 11 to the Moro Road, 10 miles (16 km) away. The Moro Road turnoff is just past the government picnic area.

"Baxter State Park" Hike (5–6 days)

With campsite reservations, IAT hikers can spend four days hiking south to north through spectacular Baxter State Park (see page 146 for details). Afterwards, leave the park through the north entrance gate (Matagammon Gatehouse). From here, it's a 1.5 mile (2.4 km) road walk to the Matagammon Wilderness Campground and Cabins ($ to $$$$, 207-446-4635, grocery store with limited camping supplies, no pay phone or laundry facilities).

From the campground, it's an 8.8-mile (14-km) road walk to a free campsite on the Sebois River maintained by the Appalachian Trail. For those wanting to continue on to Shin Brook Falls, the side-trail to the waterfalls is one mile past the AT campsite.

SHIN BROOK FALLS: A 500-metre side-trail leads to three sets of cascades. The campsite and swimming hole are below the falls.

From Shin Brook Falls, it's a 5-mile (8-km) road walk to Shin Pond Village Campground and Cabins ($$ to $$$$$, 207-528-2900, restaurant, groceries, laundry, pay phone), Mount Chase Lodge & Country Inn ($$$$$, 207-528-2183) and the Wilderness Variety Store.

After Shin Pond, follow Route 159 to Owlsboro Road, 3 miles (5 km) away. Turn left (east) on Owlsboro and follow road to Route 11, 4.5 miles (7.2 km) away. When you reach Route 11, turn left (north) and walk to the Moro Road, 4.7 miles (7.5 km) away. The Moro Road turnoff is just past the government picnic area.

Moro Road to Ludlow Road (4–6 days)

Instructions for both "Country Roads" and "Baxter State Park" hikers:

From Route 11, walk east on the Moro Road for 7.6 miles (12.1 km) until you see a yellow farmhouse with a large barn on your left. Just past the house, follow the IAT signs up the farm road to the top of hill, then 100 metres west to IAT's Roach Farm campsite. For water, follow the farm road to the edge of the woods, then south to a small pond. From Roach Farm, it's a 3.5-mile (5.6-km) road walk to Smyrna Mills.

SMYRNA MILLS: Post office, Smyrna Mills Variety Store (pizza, ice cream), no pay phone.

From Smyrna Mills, it's a 4-mile (6.4-km) road walk to a large Mennonite community. Entering the roadside store is like stepping back in time. Organic vegetables and dry goods sold here. From here, it's about 1 mile (1.6 km) farther east to the Brookside Motel and Restaurant ($$$$, 207-757-8241, air-conditioned restaurant serves home-made goodies).

From the Brookside Motel, it's less than a mile along Route 2 to the Ludlow Town Line Road. Turn left on Ludlow Town Line Road, walk a few hundred metres, then turn right on Ludlow Road. For those hiking the alternate IAT route between the Ludlow Town Line Road and Bridgewater, it's a pleasant 11-mile (17.6-km) road walk to Houlton.

There are two options between Ludlow Road and Bridgewater:

Ludlow Road to Bridgewater, IAT Route

From Ludlow Town Line Road, the IAT follows a series of unmarked country roads to Monticello, then heads north on US Route 1 to Bridgewater. To hike this route, see Maine's IAT hiking guide for details.

Ludlow Road to Bridgewater, Alternate Route (2–3 days)

Houlton to Bridgewater on the B&A Trail

Just before Houlton, you will pass Brown's Trading Post (207-532-2534), **the best hiking equipment store on the entire IAT.** For those wanting to fish the Prestile River ahead (said to be the best trout river in Maine), or do any other fishing (Meduxnekeag River and Three Brooks also ahead), buy fishing licences here. Three- and seven-day passes are available.

HOULTON (downtown): Old-fashioned American town with post office, laundromat, movie theatre, internet access at Cary Library (207 Main St.). Local sites include the infamous "Boy with Leaking Boot" sculpture and tours of the local Smith and Wesson gun factory (207-532-7966).

HOULTON (Junction Ludlow Road/US Route 1): Shiretown Inn ($$$$$, 207-532-9421), Ivey's Motor Lodge ($$$$, 207-532-4206), Traveler's Big Stop (restaurant, showers, pay phone), Stop 'N' Save (grocery store), Wal-Mart (ATM, pharmacy, camping supplies), Houlton Regional Hospital. About 1 mile (1.6 km) north of Ludlow Road on US Route 1 is My Brother's Place Campground ($, 207-532-6739, spotless shower and laundry facilities, recreation room with pool table, TV and video rentals). To hike the B&A Trail, backtrack a few hundred metres towards Houlton, then turn right (west) on the "B" Road.

From "B" Road, walk 200 metres to a rail crossing. Turn right on the road just before the tracks. Follow the road past a large building, across a large lot, to the B&A Trail. From here, it's 12 miles (19.2 km) to Monticello.

MONTICELLO: Post office, Wilde Pines Campground ($, 207-538-9004), Blue Moose

Restaurant (visible from B&A Trail), two small grocery stores.

From Monticello, follow B&A Trail north to Meduxnekeag River, 2 miles (3.2 km) away. There is a beautiful campsite on the riverbank, with good fishing. From here, it's another 7 miles (11.2 km) to Bridgewater on the B&A Trail.

BRIDGEWATER: No services in village, but there's an Irving gas station and convenience store just north of town on US Route 1 (open 24 hours). Bridgewater may lack amenities, but it does boast the world's highest outhouse. While not operational, it's still there on the second floor of the Town Hall. To see it, call friendly old-timer Mr. Eric Finnamore (IAT trail friend, contact info page 147).

End of Alternate Route

All hikers now follow B&A Trail north to Mars Hill.

From Bridgewater, it's 2.8 miles (4.5 km) on the B&A Trail to Three Brooks. There is a campsite just across the bridge (good fishing, no fires). The village of Robinsons (no services) is just past Three Brooks. From Robinsons, follow B&A Trail to Mars Hill, 4 miles (6.4 km) away. When you reach the outskirts of Mars Hill, leave the B&A Trail when you see the IGA (grocery store). Buy food here if you need it, then walk into town. When leaving, ask for directions to the Mars Hill ski hill.

MARS HILL: Post office, Midtown Motel ($$$, 207-425-6241, Al's Diner (frequented by many IAT hikers), House of Pizza, IGA (groceries), laundromat, ATM, pharmacy, Aroostook Medical Centre, internet access at Walter Hansen Memorial Library (close to post office).

Mars Hill Mountain: From town, follow IAT trail up Mars Hill Mountain. If you get lost (as I did), walk straight up the ski hill. There's an IAT shelter at the top (no water on site, bring along if you plan to stay). From here, follow IAT signs to Canada/U.S. border. From where you start walking north on the boundary strip, it's 12.8 miles (20.5 km) to the Fort Fairfield border crossing. For those wanting to camp, there's an IAT shelter midway between Mars Hill and Fort Fairfield (no water on site, but there's a stream close by).

After passing through customs, continue walking north along the international boundary to the Aroostook River, 2.5 miles (4 km) away.

Section Two: New Brunswick

Hiking Days in New Brunswick: 11–17

ACCOMMODATION PRICE GUIDE
$= 15–25	$$= 25–40	$$$= 40–55	$$$$= 55–70	$$$$$= 70+

When you reach the Aroostook River, turn right and follow Tinker Line (rail/trail) into Perth-Andover, 12 km away.

PERTH–ANDOVER: Bellevue Café and B & B ($$$$$, 506-273-3403), York's Dining Room (legendary eatery, closed Mondays), Carl's Dairy Bar (ice cream, fast-food), Southern Victoria County Historical Society Museum (cute museum in old church), Nissen's Market (bulk and organic food), United Farmers Co-op (grocery store). To get to Perth, cross bridge over the Saint John River.

PERTH–ANDOVER: Post office, Baird's Campground and Cabins ($–$$$$$, 506-273-3080, 3 km from town, no laundry facilities), Mary's Bake Shop (village hangout, excellent baked goods), Irving Station (convenience store), laundromat, Bank of Montreal (ATM), Home Hardware, several pharmacies, hospital (Hôtel Dieu St. Joseph), internet access at public library and at Community Access Centre (13 School St.).

Leaving town: From the bridge in Perth, walk 500 metres to the end of town, then follow the NB Trail (rail/trail) beside the Saint John River.

About 3 km from Perth-Andover, the NB Trail leaves the Saint John River and heads up the Tobique River. From here, it's a lovely walk beside the river to Arthurette, 20 km away.

ARTHURETTE: Arthurette General Store (506-273-2322, food, sandwiches, liquor store, pay phone). Be sure to stop at the white house near the Wagon Wheel restaurant (fast-food take-out) and visit IAT trail friend Cathy Sullivan (contact info page 147).

From Arthurette, it's 16 km to Plaster Rock on the NB Trail. Just before town, the NB Trail passes through the hamlet of Wapske, then comes out on a road. Follow the road to a bridge over the Tobique River. Cross the bridge (fabulous view), then walk up the hill to Junction 109/385.

PLASTER ROCK **(Junction 109/385):** Plaster Rock Tourist Park and Campground ($, 506-356-6077, Visitor Info Centre (free N.B. maps), Irving Station (convenience store, Kentucky Fried Chicken, Pizza Hut, ATM, pay phone), Settler's Inn and Restaurant ($$$$$, 506-356-9000). About 1 km east of Junction 109/385 (on Hwy 109), is the Tobique View Motel and Restaurant ($$$$, 506-356-2683, cheaper than Settler's Inn, laundry facilities, owner Tom Chamberlain IAT-friendly). Northern Victoria Co-op (grocery store) is a few hundred metres east of Tobique View Motel.

PLASTER ROCK **(downtown):** Post office, Greco Restaurant, Save Easy Supermarket, Royal Bank (ATM), Home Hardware, Pharmasave (pharmacy), Greer's Department Store (old-fashioned general store), Tobique Valley Hospital.

LEAVING PLASTER ROCK: If leaving from downtown, follow Hwy 108 through town, then continue 4 km (2.5 miles) to Junction 108/385. Turn right on Hwy 385 and head for Mount Carleton Provincial Park. If leaving from Junction 109/385 (near Irving Station), simply walk north on Hwy 385.

Partway through the day, you'll come to Stick's Country Store (limited groceries, ice cream, sandwiches, coffee, open 8 a.m. to 9 p.m.). From here, it's another 20 km (12.5 miles) to Riley Brook. If you can't make it to Riley Brook in one day, Blue Mountain Campground ($, 506-356-7117) is midway between Stick's Country Store and Riley Brook.

RILEY BROOK: **Last chance for supplies before Kedgwick.** Tobique Valley Campground ($$, 506-356-7258, laundry facilities), Gaston's B & B and Restaurant ($$, 506-356-9982), Riley Brook General Store (506-356-2548, groceries, camping fuel, ice cream, canoe and kayak rentals, liquor store, pay phone, owners Paul and Lucie McGuinness IAT-friendly).

From Riley Brook, it's a 10-km road walk to Black's Hunting and Fishing Camps ($, 506-356-2429), where Joe and Wanita provide reasonably priced accommodation and old-fashioned Tobique hospitality.

From Black's, it's 1.5 km to Miller Canoes, one of Canada's oldest wooden canoe-building companies. Stop in for a glass of water, a tour of the boat shop and some of Bill Miller's fine Tobique storytelling. From here, it's a further 26 km to Mount Carleton Provincial Park.

There are two options for hiking Mount Carleton Provincial Park: by foot (2 days) or with the assistance of the park staff (2 days).

Hiking Mount Carleton Provincial Park by foot (2 days)

At the park gates, reserve one night at Headwaters Campsite, then follow the park road 15 km to the Mount Carleton trailhead. Take the eastern trail up to Mount Carleton summit, 4.4 km away, then return on the western trail and camp at Headwaters Campsite, 1.2 km from the summit. The next day, follow the western trail back to the road, walk back to the park gates, turn right on Hwy 385, and you're back on the IAT.

Hiking Mount Carleton Provincial Park, assisted by park staff (2 days)

At the park gates, reserve two nights at Franquelin Campground. Arrange for park staff to pick you up at Franquelin and drive you to Mount Carleton trailhead the next morning. After all arrangements are made, walk to Franquelin Campground, 3.5 km away. After getting dropped off at the Mount Carleton trail the next day, hike up to Mount Carleton summit (4.4 km), walk across to Mount Head (3.3 km) and Mount Sagamook (2 km), then climb down Sagamook's western route to the park road. Then turn left on the road and walk back to Franquelin Campground (3.5 km/2.1 miles). The next day, walk back to the park gates, turn right on Hwy 385, and you're back on the IAT.

From Mount Carleton Provincial Park, turn left on Hwy 385 and road walk to Junction 385/180, 8 km away. Turn left on Hwy 180 and road walk to Junction 180/260, 27 km (16.9 miles) away. Turn right on Hwy 260 and road walk to Kedgwick, 18 km away. Be forewarned: it's a boring, endless road walk from Mount Carleton Provincial Park to Kedgwick. But don't lose heart, because soon you'll be ridge-walking with the caribou in Quebec.

KEDGWICK: Post office, campground (and museum) Le Musée Forestier de Kedgwick ($, 506-284-3138, 1 km north of town on Hwy 17), La Belle Etoile B & B ($$$, 506-284-2270, price includes breakfast, cheaper than O'Régal Motel, billiards, night club next door), Au P'tit Café (village hangout), Au Delice Amusant (ice cream), Bonichoix (grocery store), Co-op au Naturel (health and bulk foods), Caisse Populaire (ATM), Desjardins Quincaillerie (hardware), Famili-Prix (pharmacy), Kedgwick Sporting Goods, library, internet access at the Centre d'accès communautaire (Savoie St.). For questions about the IAT, call trail friend Maurice Simon (contact info page 147).

There are three options between Kedgwick, N.B. and Matapédia, Quebec:

From Kedgwick to Matapédia by Wilderness Trail (80 km, 5–6 days)

This option is tough going in places, but a real wilderness experience with excellent views of the Restigouche River. The trail changes from year to year, so check New Brunswick's IAT trail guide for up-to-date information (New Brunswick IAT contact info page 147).

From Kedgwick to Matapédia by the NB Trail (70 km, 3–4 days)

The NB Trail is fairly straightforward all the way to Quebec. Check New Brunswick's IAT trail guide for up-to-date information (New Brunswick IAT contact info page 147).

From Kedgwick to Matapédia by Canoeing the Restigouche River (100 km, 2–3 days)
You can rent a canoe from Arpin Canoe Restigouche, spend a few days paddling down the Restigouche River, then leave it in Matapédia, Quebec. Arpin Canoe Restigouche is located in the town of Kedgwick River, 14 km west of Kedgwick on Hwy 265 (follow the "Echo Restigouche" signs). Contact IAT trail friend André Arpin at Arpin Canoe Restigouche for details (contact info page 146).

Section Three: Quebec

(Hiking Days in Quebec: 30–40)
The Quebec section of the IAT has undergone many improvements in the last few years: hundreds of trail blazes have been erected, the path was widened and improved, and parts of the trail that were under construction — notably the Gaspé Coast and the Matane Reserve — have now been completed. Best of all, IAT Quebec produced a new set of hiking maps in 2001 (ordering info pg. 147). Between the new maps and the improved trail, hikers no longer need to worry about getting lost in Quebec.

ACCOMMODATION PRICE GUIDE				
$= 15–25	$$= 25–40	$$$= 40–55	$$$$= 55–70	$$$$$= 70+

Matapédia Valley (9–11 days)
MATAPÉDIA: Post office, Auberge de Jeunesse (youth hostel; $-$$, 418-865-2444, restaurant, laundry facilities), Motel Restigouche ($$$$, 877-865-2848), Épicerie Bujold (grocery store), Caisse Populaire (ATM), pharmacy, CLSC (medical clinic), hardware store (next to youth hostel), internet access at Bibliothèque de Matapédia (library). Be sure to contact IAT trail friend David LeBlanc before leaving town, as some sections of the Matapédia Valley are confusing (contact info page 147).

From Matapédia, it's a pretty 8-km walk through dappled maple groves to Pico Falls. After the falls, follow the trail to a parking lot. From there, turn left and follow the road to where the trail enters woods again, a few kilometres away. The trail goes through the woods for 5 km, then comes out beside the church in Saint-André-de-Restigouche (cute village, no services). Walk past the church, then turn left on the road and walk north. For those wanting to camp, there's a municipal campground 500 metres from the church. Those wanting more deluxe accommodations can stay at the Turcotte *refuge*, which is 1.5 km past the campground, on the east side of the road (200 metres off the road).

From the Turcotte *refuge*, follow the road north until you see a parking lot on your left, 2 km away. From the parking lot, follow the path 7 km through the woods to the Corbeau *refuge*.

After the Corbeau *refuge*, the IAT crosses Ruisseau Clark (stream) five times in the first 3 km. **Use caution during river crossings, particularly in May and June when water levels are high** (undo waist belt on backpack, wear shoes, carry a walking stick). After the fifth river crossing, follow the trail to an old road, then follow the signs to the Quartz *refuge*, 14 km away.

From the Quartz *refuge*, follow the path behind the shelter, along the crest of a hill, then down to the Assemetquagan River again, 5.8 km away. Wade across the Assemetquagan, then climb the opposite riverbank and follow the path up the Creux River valley. In 4.9 km, the path will descend to the Creux River. Wade across, then follow the path through the wild blueberry fields to the second Creux River crossing, 3.3 km away. Cross the bridge and walk 200 metres to the Ruisseau Creux campsite and *refuge*. From here, it's 12 km to the village of Sainte-Marguerite.

SAINTE-MARGUERITE: Post office, convenience store.

From Sainte-Marguerite, the IAT follows country roads to Causapscal, 17.9 km away. Camping Municipal St. Jacques ($, 418-756-5621, laundry facilities, pay phone) is on the far side of town, on Hwy 132.

CAUSAPSCAL: Post office, several hotels, plenty of restaurants (good café across from campground), Marché Richelieu (grocery store), laundromat, Caisse Populaire (ATM), Raymond Bellavance et fils (hardware store), Pharmacie Albert Lévesque (pharmacy), CLSC (medical clinic, close to campground). For sight-seeing, visit Site Historique Matamajaw, a museum that celebrates the town's glory days of Atlantic salmon sport fishing (French-only exhibits).

From Causapscal, the IAT leaves from behind Camping Municipal St. Jacques. Turn left on the path and follow the trail 10.4 km to the Causapscal River. Turn left at the river and follow the path 6.6 km to Les Chutes campsite.

From Les Chutes, follow the path past the salmon pool and observation area. After admiring the salmon, follow the IAT signs to the Chute à Philomène, 15.3 km away. From Philomène, it's 2.5 km to the village of Saint-Alexandre-des-Lacs.

SAINT-ALEXANDRE-DES-LACS: Post office, Dépanneur des Lacs (convenience store with limited groceries), Bar l'Entre-Quatre (tavern).

From Saint-Alexandre-des-Lacs, follow the IAT 4.5 km to Rang Saint-Napoléon (road). Follow Rang Saint-Napoléon to Hwy 195, 2.5 km away. For those wanting to re-supply in Amqui, turn left on Hwy 195 and walk into town, 2 km away. Camping d'Amqui ($, 418-629-3433, laundry facilities, pedal boats, heated pool and croquet) is a full-service campground, but unfortunately it's 4 km from town, on Hwy 132.

AMQUI: Post office, Hotel Amqui ($, 418-629-4575, run-down but clean and quaint), several restaurants (everything from fast-food to haute cuisine), two large grocery stores (Provigo and GP), laundromat, Caisse Populaire (ATM), Amqui BMR (camping fuel), Uniprix (pharmacy), Hart's (department store), CLSC (medical clinic), Amqui Hospital, internet access at Bibliothèque d'Amqui (library).

From Amqui, walk back to Rang Saint-Napoléon and pick up the IAT again on the opposite side of Hwy 195. Follow the road for 500 metres, watching for IAT signs on your right. When you find the path, follow it 1 km to the Champs campsite. From Champs, follow the trail 9.2 km to Camp Sable-Chaud, a children's summer camp near Lac Matapédia. From Sable-Chaud, it's another 10.7 km to the Trois Soeurs *refuge* and campsite (no water on site, bring some from Lac Matapédia if you stay here). From Trois Soeurs, it's 12.5 km to the village of Saint-Vianney.

SAINT-VIANNEY: **Last chance to re-supply before Matane Reserve and Parc de la Gaspésie.** Post office, grocery store, restaurant.

From Saint-Vianney, follow IAT signs from town, through the woods, then out to Hwy 195, approx. 10.2 km away. When you reach the road, you'll see Camp Tamagodi ($-$$, 418 224 3340, camping, motel, restaurant, owner Dennis Lord IAT-friendly) a short distance away. From here it's a 4.6-km road walk to the Poste John information booth in the Matane Reserve.

Matane Reserve (6–8 days)

Hikers must reserve campsites and *refuges* before travelling through the Matane Reserve and the Parc de la Gaspésie. Bookings can be made in advance by calling SEPAQ (see page 146) or in person at the Matane Reserve.

From Poste John, the IAT follows the Matane River for 1.9 km, then climbs out of the valley and follows the escarpment to Le Ruisseau des Pitounes campsite, 9.8 km away. From there, it's an easy day's hike to the Lac Tombereau campsite, 13.6 km away. The next day's hike takes you 14 km to the Lac Matane campsite.

It's a gruelling 19.8-km hike from the Lac Matane campsite to the summit of Mont Blanc, with some astonishing panoramic views of logging devastation along the way. At the top is a snug little cabin where hikers can stay free of charge (not owned by SEPAQ). There's no water on site, but you'll find a *point d'eau* (water source) a short distance from the summit.

It's another challenging day from the Mont Blanc *refuge* to the Petit Sault campsite, 20.1 km away. Points of interest include Mont Nicol-Albert (spectacular views from the summit) and the Beaulieu Chutes (three kilometres of tumbling waterfalls). NOTE: The trail down the Beaulieu Chutes is steep, narrow and slippery. If you arrive late in the day, camp at the top of the falls and walk down in the morning.

Re-supplying between the Matane Reserve and the Parc de la Gaspésie

If you need to re-supply before entering the Parc de la Gaspésie, you can hitchhike north on the Cap-Chat Road to the village of Cap-Chat, 40 km away. Cap-Chat has most services, including a post office, Motel/Camping Fleur de Lys ($-$$, 418-786-5518, restaurant, internet access, laundromat close by), 3 grocery stores, a Caisse Populaire (ATM), 2 hardware stores, and a CLSC (medical clinic). To return to the IAT, hitch-hike or take a taxi (Taxi 300, 418-763-2630, approx. $70). When you return, pick up the trail on the opposite side of Cap-Chat Road.

The trail between the Petit Sault campsite and Mont Logan *refuge* is one of the prettiest days on the entire IAT. Leaving the campsite, turn left on the Cap-Chat Road and walk 1.7 km to where the IAT enters the woods again. Follow the path to the Chute Hélène side-trail, approx. 4 km away. After cooling off in the spray of this impressive 70-metre waterfall, retrace your steps back to the main trail, then follow the path 6 km to Mont Collins. The trail up Mont Collins is brutal, but the spectacular ridge walk across to Mont Matawees more than makes up for it. From Matawees, the trail descends into a valley, then starts climbing Mont Fortin. Soon hikers will pass a sign welcoming them to the Parc de la Gaspésie. This is the end of the Matane Reserve. From here, it's a gorgeous walk up the hill and across a knife-edged ridge across to Mont Logan.

Parc de la Gaspésie (4–6 days)

After the rigours of hiking the Matane Reserve, crossing the Parc de la Gaspésie, with its gently graded trails and deluxe *refuges*, is like taking a walk in the park.

From Mont Logan *refuge*, follow the trail 12 km to the Carouge *refuge*. Those wanting to do some moose watching can stay here for the night. Those wanting a full day of hiking can continue on to Le Huard *refuge*, 8.7 km away.

From the Huard refuge, follow the trail 25.8 km to Lac Cascapédia. The scenery in this section of the trail is gorgeous, particularly on the Pic l'Aube side-trail. SEPAQ campsites and *refuges* are available at Lac Cascapédia.

From Lac Cascapédia, it's a long but spectacular walk to the Gîte du Mont-Albert (on Hwy 299), 28 km away. Watch for rare alpine plants and caribou on top of Mont-Albert. When the trail splits at the east end of the summit, take the Vallée Trail down the valley (prettier than the Montée trail), past the Lac du Diable (Devil Lake), then down to Hwy 299. From here, turn right for Camping Mont-Albert (showers, laundry facilities, SEPAQ *refuges* available) or left for the Gîte du Mont-Albert ($$$$$, 418-763-2288). If you're unwilling to blow $75 on dinner at the Gîte, there's a snack bar (poutine! hot dogs! ice-cold Coke!) a short distance from the Gîte.

Re-supplying from within the Parc de la Gaspésie

If you need to re-supply before continuing east through the park, you can go to Sainte-Anne-des-Monts, 40 km away. Sainte-Anne has all services, including post office, International Youth Hostel ($, 418-763-1555), two grocery stores, laundromat, Caisse Populaire (ATM), hardware store, CLSC (medical clinic), internet access at the local library. Shuttles for Saint-Anne leave daily from Parc de la Gaspésie's Interpretation Centre.

From Camping Mont-Albert, it's a pleasant 4- to 5-hour walk to the Tetras *refuge,* 16.2 km away. From here, the trail climbs up and over Mont Jacques-Cartier (watch for caribou!), then descends 13 km to Camping du Mont Jacques-Cartier (SEPAQ *refuges* are also available).

Upper Gaspé (2–3 days)

From Camping du Mont Jacques-Cartier, it's 13.7 km to Les Cabourons *refuge* and a farther 21.3 km to Camping Mont-Saint-Pierre ($, 418-797-2951).

MONT–SAINT–PIERRE: Post office, Hôtel Mont-Saint-Pierre ($$, 418-797-2202, restaurant, laundry facilities, owner Raymond IAT-friendly), Marché Cloutier (grocery store), Caisse Populaire (ATM), internet access at Bibliothèque du Mont-Saint-Pierre (library).

From the town of Mont-Saint-Pierre, it's a pleasant walk up and over Mont Saint-Pierre, then along Hwy 132 to Gros-Morne, 21.6 km away. There are great views of the wind-lashed sea.

GROS–MORNE: Limited groceries at Dépanneur Chez Louise.

Leaving Gros-Morne, the trail heads up the Gros-Morne River valley, then turns east and towards the Manche-d'Épée River, 8.8 km away. The trail crosses the river, climbs sharply for a few kilometres, then turns east and heads towards Madeleine-Centre, 12.9 km away.

MADELEINE–CENTRE: Post office, Camping Bel-Aire, Hôtel/Motel Rocher ($$$, 1-800-391-2425, restaurant, laundry facilities, owner Leopold Rocher IAT-friendly), Épicier Fournier (grocery, ATM), internet access at the Bibliothèque du Madeleine-Centre (library).

From Madeleine-Centre, it's a 2-km road walk to the village of Rivière-la-Madeleine (be sure to stop at Restaurant Chez Mamie for something to eat). Midway between the two villages is a lighthouse with a commercial campground and a coffee shop with internet access. From the lighthouse, it's 9.2 km to the Grand-Sault campsite.

Gaspé Coast (6–8 days)

Grand-Sault Fish Ladder: From the Grand-Sault campsite, it's a 3-km side-trip to the world's longest underground fish ladder.

From the Grand-Sault campsite, the trail passes a series of lakes then comes out on Hwy 132, 9 km away. Turn right (east) on Hwy 132 and road walk 9.9 km to Grande-Vallée.

GRANDE-VALLÉE: Post office, Camping Au Soleil Couchant ($, 418-393-2489, laundry facilities), Motel-Restaurant La Marée-Haute ($$$, 418-393-3008), two grocery stores, Caisse Populaire (ATM), hardware store, pharmacy, CLSC (medical clinic, open 24 hours), internet access at the Bibliothèque de Grande-Vallée (library).

Pick up the IAT at the east end of Grande-Vallée. From here, the trail follows the water's edge to Petite-Vallée, 7.1 km away. After Petite-Vallée, keep walking east along the beach. After a few hours, start watching for IAT signs on your right. When you find the trail, follow it 11 km to Les Terrasses campsite.

From Les Terrasses campsite, the trail passes through a forest, crosses a few logging roads, descends into a valley, then comes out on a road. Turn right (south) on the road and follow the signs to Les Cascades *refuge*, 11.5 km away.

From Les Cascades, follow the path to the Cloridorme village turnoff, 2.5 km away. From the intersection, hikers have two options: either hike 3 km down to Cloridorme, then follow Hwy 132 east to Saint-Yvon, or keep following the trail along the top of the hill, then descend to Saint-Yvon, 9 km away. From Saint-Yvon, the trail follows the water's edge for 5 km to l'Anse-à-l'Étang From here, it's another 8.4 km to La Chute campsite.

From La Chute campsite, continue walking east along the top of the escarpment until you reach a steep ravine. Follow the trail north down the ravine to Hwy 132. Turn right on the road, walk a few hundred metres, then turn left and follow the trail straight up the hill (the trail builders apologize for the steep slope — they had to follow the survey line). From the top of the hill, follow the trail to Pointe-à-la-Renommée lighthouse. After visiting this jet-setting lighthouse (you'll understand once you get there), continue walking east to the Zéphir *refuge* (magnificent setting), a short distance away. From here, it's another 4 km to L'Anse-à-Valleau.

L'ANSE-À-VALLEAU: Post office, Auberge des Ancêtres ($$$, 418-269-3371, camping, restaurant, laundry facilities, owner Mr. Boulay IAT-friendly).

From L'Anse-à-Valleau, follow the old road behind the Auberge des Ancêtres to where the trail enters the woods again. When you find the trail, follow it to the Saint-Maurice-de-l'Échouerie junction, 5 km away (pay close attention to IAT trail markers, as there are ATV trails through here too). From the junction, keep following the path for 3 km to Les Carrières campsite.

From Les Carrières, follow the trail 9 km to the L'Érablière *refuge*. From here, follow the trail to a power line a few kilometres away, then follow the power line down to Hwy 197. Those wanting a restaurant meal and a good night's sleep before tackling Forillon can rent a tepee at Parc de la Vallée Soleil ($$$, 1-877-313-7373, on Hwy 132, close to trail). Those wanting a full hiking day can keep following the IAT to Forillon National Park's western entrance, 2.2 km away.

Forillon National Park (2 days)

No reservations are required for Forillon National Park. IAT hikers can camp at back-country campsites for free.

From the park's western entrance, take the path 11.4 km through the woods to the campsite near Lac de Penouille. From here, follow the trail to a bike path, 4.4 km away. Cross the bike path and continue east to the Les Crêtes campsite, another 5.4 km.

From Les Crêtes, follow the path through woods to where Hwy 132 cuts through the park, 7.3 km away. Cross Hwy 132 and pick up the trail on the opposite side of the road. Follow the path through the woods to Mont Saint-Alban junction, 4.2 km away. Turning left at the junction brings you to Mont Saint-Alban lookout (do NOT miss the spectacular view in your haste to complete your IAT hike), and then the Grande-Grave National Historic Site. From Grande-Grave, it's approx. 8 km to Cap Gaspé and the end of the IAT.

GASPÉ: Post office, Camping Fort Ramsay ($, 418-368-5094, 3 km out of town towards Forillon), Motel Adams ($$$$, 418-368-2244, bus station in hotel lobby, restaurant, night club downstairs), several grocery stores (Provigo close to Motel Adams), laundromat, several banks with ATM, hardware store, pharmacy, CLSC (medical clinic), Centre hospitalier de Gaspé (hospital).

Quick-Look Chart

SERVICES			
PO	Post office	HS	Hardware Store
C	Camping	P	Pharmacy
A	Accommodation	MC	Medical Clinic
	(cabins, hotels/motels, *refuges*)	H	Hospital
R	Restaurant	I	Internet Access
G	Groceries	☉	SEPAQ (campsites and *refuges*
L	Laundromat		maintained by Quebec government)
ATM	Automatic teller machine		

TRAIL SURFACES			
W	Wilderness Trail	V	Road used by vehicular traffic
R/T	Rail/Trail	S	Seashore Trail
ATV	Backcountry trail used by		
	all-terrain vehicles		

Note that the names of towns and villages appear in SMALL CAPITALS.

MAINE

LOCATION	SERVICES	DISTANCE (BETWEEN)		DISTANCE (TOTAL)		TRAIL
		MILES	KM	MILES	KM	SURFACE
(On "Country Roads" trail)						
Mount Katahdin (summit)		0	0	0	0	W
Abol Bridge Campground	C, G	15	24	15	24	W, V
MILLINOCKET	PO, C, A, R, G, L, ATM, HS, P, H, I	20.8	33.3	35.8	57.3	V
Sherman (Junction)	A, R	35	56	70.8	113.3	V
PATTEN	PO, A, R, G, L, ATM, HS, P, MC, I	9	14.4	79.8	127.7	V
SMYRNA MILLS	PO, G	21.1	33.7	100.9	161.4	V
HOULTON	PO, C, A, R,G, L, ATM, HS, P, H, I	17	27.2	117.9	188.6	V
MONTICELLO	PO, C, R, G	12	19.2	129.9	207.8	R/T
(On the "Alternate Route")						
Bridgewater	G	9	14.4	138.9	222.2	R/T
MARS HILL	PO, A, R, G, L, ATM, P, MC, I	7.3	11.7	146.2	233.9	R/T
Fort Fairfield Border Crossing		20	32	166.2	265.9	W, ATV

NEW BRUNSWICK

LOCATION	SERVICES	DISTANCE (BETWEEN)		DISTANCE (TOTAL)		TRAIL
		MILES	KM	MILES	KM	SURFACE
Aroostook River		2.5	4	2.5	4	ATV
PERTH–ANDOVER	PO, C, A, R, G, L, ATM, HS, P, H, I	7.5	12	10	16	R/T
Arthurette	G	14.4	23	24.4	39	R/T
PLASTER ROCK	PO, C, A, R, G, ATM, HS, P, H	10	16	34.4	55	R/T, V
Stick's Store	R, G	11.9	19	46.3	74	V
Riley Brook	C, A, R, G	12.5	20	58.8	94	V
Black's Hunting and Fishing Camps	A	6.25	10	65	104	V
Mount Carleton Provincial Park	C	17.2	27.5	82.2	131.5	V
Junction 385/180		5	8	87.2	139.5	V
Junction 180/260		16.9	27	104.1	166.5	V
KEDGWICK	PO, C, A, R, G, ATM, HS, P, I	11.25	18	115.4	184.5	R/T
From Kedgwick to Matapédia on NB Trail		44	70	159.4	254.5	R/T, V

QUEBEC

For the section below, refer to IAT Quebec's **"Matapédia Valley"** map.

LOCATION	SERVICES	DISTANCE (BETWEEN)		DISTANCE (TOTAL)		TRAIL
		MILES	KM	MILES	KM	SURFACE
MATAPÉDIA	PO, C, A, R, G, ATM, HS, P, MC, I	0	0	0	0	
Saint-André-de-Restigouche	C	9.4	15	9.4	15	W
⊙ "Turcotte" *refuge*	A	1.3	2	10.7	17	
⊙ "Corbeau" *refuge*	A	5.6	9	16.3	26	W, V
⊙ "Quartz" *refuge*	A	10.6	17	26.9	43	W, ATV
⊙ "Le Ruisseau Creux" campsite and *refuge*	C, A	8.8	14	35.7	57	W
SAINTE–MARGUERITE	PO, G	7.5	12	43.2	69	W, ATV, V
CAUSAPSCAL	PO, C, A, R, G, L, ATM, HS, P, MC	11.2	17.9	54.4	86.9	V
⊙ "Les Chutes" campsite	C	10.6	17	65	103.9	W, V
SAINT–ALEXANDRE–DES–LACS	PO, G	11.1	17.8	76.1	121.7	W, V
AMQUI	PO, C, A, R, G, L, ATM, HS, P, MC, H, I	5.6	9	81.7	130.7	W, V

For the section below, refer to IAT Quebec's **"Matane Wildlife Reserve"** map.

LOCATION	SERVICES	DISTANCE (BETWEEN)		DISTANCE (TOTAL)		TRAIL
		MILES	KM	MILES	KM	SURFACE
⊙ "Trois Soeurs" refuge and campsite	C	14.5	23.3	96.2	154	W, V
SAINT-VIANNEY	PO, G, R	7.8	12.5	104	166.5	W, V
Camp Tamagodi	C, A, R	6.4	10.2	110.4	176.7	V
Matane Reserve (Poste John)	C	2.9	4.6	113.3	181.3	W, V
⊙ "Le Ruisseau des Pitounes" campsite	C	7.3	11.7	120.6	193	W
⊙ "Lac Tombereau" campsite	C	8.5	13.6	129.1	206.6	W
⊙ "Lac Matane" campsite	C	8.8	14	137.9	220.6	W
Mont Blanc refuge	A	12.4	19.8	150.3	240.4	W
⊙ "Petit Sault" campsite	C	12.5	20.1	162.8	260.5	W
Mont Logan refuge	A	11.9	19.1	174.7	279.6	W, V

For the section below, refer to the **Parc de la Gaspésie's 1:75,000 topographic map.**

LOCATION	SERVICES	DISTANCE (BETWEEN)		DISTANCE (TOTAL)		TRAIL
		MILES	KM	MILES	KM	SURFACE
⊙ "Le Huard" refuge	A	12.9	20.7	187.6	300.3	W, V
⊙ Lac Cascapédia	C, A	16.1	25.8	203.7	326.1	W
⊙ Camping Mont-Albert	C, A	17.5	28	221.2	354.1	W
⊙ "Le Tetras" refuge	A	10.1	16.2	231.3	370.3	W
⊙ Camping du Mont Jacques-Cartier	C, A	8.1	13	239.4	383.3	W

For the section below, refer to IAT Quebec's **"Upper Gaspé"** map.

LOCATION	SERVICES	DISTANCE (BETWEEN)		DISTANCE (TOTAL)		TRAIL
		MILES	KM	MILES	KM	SURFACE
⊙ "Les Cabourons" refuge	A	8.5	13.7	247.9	397	W, V
Camping Mont-Saint-Pierre	C	13.3	21.3	261.2	418.3	W, V
MONT-SAINT-PIERRE	PO, A, R, G, L, ATM, I	2.1	3.4	263.3	421.7	W, V
Gros-Morne	G	13.5	21.6	276.8	443.3	V, ATV
MADELEINE-CENTRE	PO, C, A, R, G, L, ATM, I	13.5	21.7	290.3	465	W

For the section below, refer to IAT Quebec's **"Gaspé Coast Sector"** map.

| LOCATION | SERVICES | DISTANCE (BETWEEN) | | DISTANCE (TOTAL) | | TRAIL |
		MILES	KM	MILES	KM	SURFACE
⊙ "Grand Sault" campsite	C	7	11.2	297.3	476.2	W, V
GRANDE-VALLÉE	PO, C, A, R, G, L, ATM, HS, P, MC, I	11.8	18.9	309.1	495.1	W, V
⊙ "Les Terrasses" campsite	C	11.3	18.1	320.4	513.2	W, S
⊙ "Les Cascades" *refuge*	A	7.1	11.5	327.5	524.7	W
⊙ "La Chute" campsite	C	15.5	24.8	343	549.5	W, V, S
⊙ "Zéphir" *refuge*	A	5.1	8.3	348.1	557.8	W, V, S
L'Anse-à-Valleau	C, A, R, L, PO	2.5	4	350.6	557.8	S
⊙ "Les Carrières" campsite	C	5	8	355.6	561.8	W, V
Parc de la Vallée Soleil	C, R	10.9	17.4	366.5	587.2	W, ATV

For the section below, refer to "The Trails of Forillon National Park" map.

| LOCATION | SERVICES | DISTANCE (BETWEEN) | | DISTANCE (TOTAL) | | TRAIL |
		MILES	KM	MILES	KM	SURFACE
Forillon National Park (western entrance)		1.4	2.2	367.9	589.4	W
"Les Crêtes" campsite	C	13.25	21.2	381.1	610.6	W
Cap-Gaspé and end of IAT	C	15.8	25.4	396.9	636	W, S
GASPÉ	PO, C, A, R, G, L, ATM, HS, P, MC, H					

An Invitation For All IAT Hikers

WOULD YOU LIKE TO HELP KEEP THE ESSENTIAL GUIDE UP-TO-DATE?

I've done my best to make this guide as accurate as possible, but there may be errors here and there, and time eventually makes all travel guides obsolete. The best way to keep the Essential Guide accurate is through the internet. I've taken the first step by posting it on the Web at **www.iatguide.ca**. Now I need your help: if you spot inaccuracies in the text, if you think something should be added, if some of the information has changed, or if you have suggestions for improving this guide, please also let me know. If we work at this together, we can keep the web version of the Essential Guide accurate and up-to-date for years to come.

Please e-mail your corrections and comments to mail@iatguide.ca. In addition to offering on-line access to the Essential Guide, www.iatguide.ca is an essential resource for locating IAT maps, guides, updated trail information, discussion groups and IAT hiking events, as well being a cheerful source of advice, encouragement and inspiration for anyone planning (or dreaming!) of hiking the IAT.

Suggested Reading

Books

THE APPALACHIAN TRAIL

Bruce, Dan "Wingfoot." *The Thru-hiker's Handbook: #1 Guide for Long-Distance Hikes on the Appalachian Trail.* Hot Springs, NC: Center for Appalachian Trail Studies, 2001.

Bryson, Bill. *A Walk in the Woods.* Toronto: Doubleday Canada, 1998. A very funny book about hiking the Appalachian Trail. A great trail book.

Chase, Jim. *Backpacker Magazine's Guide to the Appalachian Trail.* Harrisburg, PA: Stackpole Books, 1989.

Eberhart, M.J. *Ten Million Steps.* Helena, Mont.: Sky House, 2000.

Luxenberg, Larry. *Walking the Appalachian Trail.* Mechanicsburg, PA: Stackpole Books, 1994.

BACKPACKING

Fleming, June. *The Well-Fed Backpacker.* New York: Vintage, 1986. This helpful how-to book covers menu-planning, food packing, hiking recipes and cooking on the trail.

Fletcher, Colin. *The Complete Walker III: The Joys and Techniques of Hiking.* New York: Knopf, 1970. The grand-daddy of hiking encyclopaedias, now in its third edition. Full of sage advice like "The hottest fire comes from small sticks," "Dirty socks can cause abrasions faster" and "Walking sticks are good for checking bushes for snakes."

Herrero, Stephen. *Bear Attacks: Their Causes and Avoidance.* New York: Lyons & Burford, 1988. In this riveting page-turner the author reviews every bear attack that occurred in North America between 1900 and 1980. Tips on how to avoid bear confrontations are also included.

Meyer, Kathleen. *How to Shit in the Woods: An Environmentally Sound Approach to a Lost Art*. 2nd ed. Berkley: Ten Speed Press, 1994. The perfect book for those who don't know how to do it, and aren't sure who to ask. This funny how-to book covers everything from portable potties to crotch-accessible clothing for women, from the "Plight of the solo poop-packer" to paper-less techniques.

Townsend, Chris. *The Advanced Backpacker: A Handbook for Year-Round, Long-Distance Hiking*. Camden, ME: Ragged Mountain Press, 2001. The author has crammed 35,000 kilometres of hiking experience into this excellent how-to book. If you read only one book in preparation for your IAT hike, make it this one.

MAINE

Clark, Charles E. *Maine: A Bicentennial History*. New York: Norton, 1997. Good general interest history text.

Rolde, Neil. *The Baxters of Maine: Downeast Visionaries.* Gardiner, ME: Tilbury House, 1997. A detailed historical account of Maine's most famous family.

Wallach, Bret. *At Odds With Progress: Americans and Conservation*. Tucson: University of Arizona Press, 1991. A dissertation on the successes and failures of the American conservation movement. Percival Baxter is mentioned.

NEW BRUNSWICK

McLeod, Carol. *Glimpses into New Brunswick History.* Hantsport, N.S.: Lancelot Press, 1984. New Brunswick history.

Peck, Mary. *The Bitter with the Sweet: New Brunswick 1604–1984.* Tantallon, N.S.: Four East Publications, 1983. New Brunswick history, including an excellent account of the region's early logging practices.

Shaw, Marilyn. *Mount Carleton Wilderness: New Brunswick's Unknown North*. Fredericton, N.B.: Goose Lane Editions, 1987. Well-written history of a fascinating but forgotten region. The "Murder on the Tobique" story is mentioned.

Soucoup, Dan. *Historic New Brunswick*. East Lawrencetown, N.S.: Pottersfield Press, 1997. Excellent book on New Brunswick history.

Toner, Peter, ed. *New Ireland Remembered: Historical Essays on the Irish in New Brunswick*. Fredericton: New Ireland Press, 1988. A thorough survey of New Brunswick's early Irish history.

Whitney Thompson, Colleen. *Roads to Remember: An Insider's Guide to New Brunswick*. Fredericton: Goose Lane Editions, 1994. A cheerfully written, well-researched New Brunswick guide book.

Wilbur, Richard. *The Rise of French New Brunswick*. Halifax: Formac Publishing, 1989. New Brunswick's early Acadian history.

QUEBEC

Clarke, John. *Sketches of Gaspé*. Albany, N.Y.: J. B. Lyon, 1908. Turn-of-the-century book about the Gaspé Peninsula, written in a wonderfully florid style.

Davies, Blodwen. *Gaspé: Land of History and Romance*. Toronto: Ambassador Books, 1949. Well-written historical account of Quebec's Gaspé Peninsula.

Department of Highways and Mines. *The Gaspé Peninsula*. Quebec, 1930. Somewhat dated guide book on Quebec's Gaspé Peninsula.

Jepson, Tim et al. *Canada*. London: Rough Guides, 2001. Excellent section on Quebec.

Remillard, Francois et al. *Québec 2001*. Montreal: Ulysses, 2001. Good general purpose guide book on the province.

Smith, Olive Willett. *Gaspé the Romantique*. New York: Crowell, 1936. Historical guide book on the Gaspé Peninsula.

Articles

"Irving." *Canadian Business Magazine*. 30 July 1999.

Kekacks, Andy. "International Appalachian Trail Stretches into Canada." *Northern Woodlands Magazine*, spring 2000.

Kesich, Gregory. "A Walk Beyond the Border." *Portland Press Herald*, 1 October 2000.

Mann, Paul. "Trek Through to the True End of the Appalachian Mountains." *www.gorp.com*. 21 July 2001.

Sharp, David. "Earl Shaffer [sic] Completes Thru-Hike." *Associated Press*, 21 October 1998.

"Signs of the Times." *Montreal Gazette*. 11 November 2000.

Pamphlets

Edwards, Henry. *The Thru-Hiker's Companion Guide to the IAT*. IAT Maine, 2000.

Forillon Visitor's Guide, 2000. Parks Canada, 2000.

Katahdin Area Visitor Guide. Katahdin Area Chamber of Commerce, 2000.

Parc de la Gaspésie: Une Mer de Montagnes. Parc Ami Chic Choc. 1990.

The Restigouche River. Government of New Brunswick, 1995.

Wildflowers of New Brunswick. Government of New Brunswick, 1986.

Acknowledgements

Acknowledgements must begin with my father, who tirelessly scoured this text for leading clauses, shifting tenses, dangling modifiers and plain old flabby thinking. More importantly, he told me he liked the book — which for me is about the highest praise there is.

In writing this book, I'm also grateful for the help of IAT founder Richard B. ("Dick") Anderson (who became very familiar with the sentence "Just one more question, really"); Mel Fitton, Bob Melville, André Fornier and Maurice Simon of IAT New Brunswick; Jocelyne De Champlain, Viateur De Champlain, Jean-Claude Bouchard and Jacques Chartier of IAT Quebec; Joan Hookwater at Baxter State Park; L. Blanchard at Mount Carlton Provincial Park; Jean-Philippe Chartrand at the Parc de la Gaspésie; Jean-Guy Chavarie at Forillon National Park; the terrific John Watling; and Scott Steedman, my ever-encouraging editor at Raincoast Books.

A heartfelt thank-you also to the Parc de la Gaspésie and Forillion National Park for allowing me to reproduce several images from their photo collections in this book.

I am also very grateful to the many people who showered me with kindness, food and encouragement as I hiked the IAT: Martin Segal, Abelina Gorham, Dave and Debbie Burpee, Connie Miguel, John Camilleri (Johnny Down Under), Joyce Craig, Bob and Bernice Miller, Bill Miller, Wilma Miller, André Arpin, David LeBlanc, and last but not least, the two jolly East Germans who picked me up after I'd finished hiking the trail, then drove forty kilometres out of their way to drop me off, weaving all over the road, singing songs and plying me with cigarettes.

Monique Dykstra is a Montreal-based photographer and writer whose work has appeared in various national and international publications, including *GEO*, *Alaska Magazine*, *Canoe and Kayak*, *Imperial Oil Review* and *Canadian Inflight Magazine*. She has been responsible for *Eye on Montreal*, a regular column in the *Gazette* featuring her portraits of extraordinary people, since 1998. Her previous book, *My Heart on the Yukon River: Portraits from Alaska and the Yukon* (Washington State University Press, 1997), was a similar mix of photos and stories.

ALSO AVAILABLE FROM RAINCOAST IN THE POPULAR JOURNEYS SERIES:

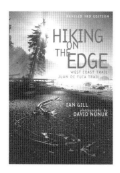

Hiking on the Edge ★ Revised Third Edition
Ian Gill, photographs by **David Nunuk**
A journey in pictures and words along the West Coast Trail.
With a revised section on the Juan de Fuca Marine Trail and updated
information, this book is the definitive resource for both the armchair
traveller and veteran hiker interested in venturing to the western
edge of British Columbia's Vancouver Island.
1-55192-505-2 • $29.95 CDN / $19.95 US

Haida Gwaii
Ian Gill, photographs by **David Nunuk**
Bill Reid once called Haida Gwaii, or the Queen Charlotte
Islands, the "Shining Islands." This bestselling travelogue shows
just why these fabled islands on the western edge of Canada
have fascinated and enchanted people for thousands of years.
1-55192-068-9 • $29.95 CDN / $19.95 US

Paddling Through Time
Joanna Streetly, photographs by **Adrian Dorst**
With its spectacular bays and beaches, Clayoquot Sound has enthralled
everyone privileged to experience it, from the First Nations people
and European explorers to today's whale-watchers and tourists. In this
book, two residents bring insiders' knowledge to their account of a
week-long kayak trip through the sound.
1-55192-278-9 • $29.95 CDN / $19.95 US

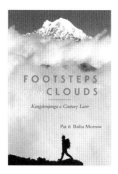

Footsteps in the Clouds
Baiba and Pat Morrow
In 1899, a team of adventurers including Italian photographer
Vittorio Sella climbed the sacred Himalayan peak of
Kangchenjunga, the world's third highest mountain. A century
later Pat Morrow, the first Canadian to scale Everest, teamed
up with his wife Baiba to follow in Sella's footstep. This is
their story, in pictures and words.
1-55192-226-6 • $26.95 CDN / $18.95 US